GREATER
FOOL

GREATER FOOL

THE TROUBLED FUTURE OF REAL ESTATE

GARTH TURNER

KEY PORTER BOOKS

Library and Archives Canada Cataloguing in Publication

Turner, Garth
  Greater Fool : the troubled future of real estate / Garth Turner.

ISBN 978-1-55470-108-7

  1. Real estate investment—Canada—Forecasting. 2. Real property—Canada. I. Title.

HD1379.T875 2008   332.63'24   C2008-900735-2

ONTARIO ARTS COUNCIL
CONSEIL DES ARTS DE L'ONTARIO

The publisher gratefully acknowledges the support of the Canada Council for the Arts
and the Ontario Arts Council for its publishing program. We acknowledge the support of
the Government of Ontario through the Ontario Media Development Corporation's
Ontario Book Initiative.

We acknowledge the financial support of the Government of Canada through the Book
Publishing Industry Development Program (BPIDP) for our publishing activities.

Key Porter Books Limited
Six Adelaide Street East, Tenth Floor
Toronto, Ontario
Canada M5C 1H6

www.keyporter.com

Text design: Jean Lightfoot Peters
Electronic formatting: Jean Lightfoot Peters

Printed and bound in Canada

08 09 10 11 12 5 4 3 2 1

CONTENTS

INTRODUCTION

THE GRAVEL PARKING lot outside the presentation centre near Toronto is jammed most weekends. Every few minutes another young couple arrive, head inside and buy a house. Unbuilt, unseen, on streets yet to be carved from the farm field out back, the homes will be huge and expensive. Most of the buyers have little money—just a few thousand dollars. But they buy anyway. Many of them sign up for mortgages covering 98 per cent of the cost. They're ecstatic.

Thousands of kilometres west, another couple watches as the last of the furniture's off-loaded. They embrace, white hair luminous in the sunshine, Okanagan Lake in the distance. Waterfront homes here have doubled in value. The purchase took all the money from the last house, and most of their mutual fund savings, but this is a happy day. They will spend their best years here, then sell, of course, and use the profits to finance the rest of their lives.

Every hour of each day, Canadians make decisions about real estate they may come to bitterly regret. They believe investing in a home is a riskless act with a predictable outcome. As a people, we've bought into a myth of ever-rising home prices, which is reinforced daily by a self-serving industry and a pliant media. So hooked are we, that four of every five dollars the average family has now is buried in a single asset, on a single street, in a single town.

When it comes to granite counters, stainless steel appliances and paving stones we seem blind to threats the world now holds. While the market in Saskatoon and North York boomed, we paid scant attention to two million Americans losing their homes, while US real estate prices took the worst drop since the Great Depression. While oil raced to a historic high price and science reeled at climate change, we bought ever-larger and costly homes in distant, car-clogged subdivisions. And while nine million home-owning baby boomers watched stock markets with suspicion, they sat on wealth in four-bedroom houses that may never find buyers.

How did we allow this obsession to grip us so? Why have we put so much of our precious wealth into assets that are by every measure over-inflated and likely to tumble in value? How can millions of us believe that the real estate boom can last forever, in a spin of rising prices, when no boom has ever done so before?

Too many Canadians are living a dream, while the lives of tens of millions of their American neighbours have been shattered in a real estate nightmare. Ever-increasing debt loads have masked the fact that average families can no longer afford average homes. When bungalows in Vancouver cost $900,000 and resale homes with no parking in midtown Toronto are $1 million, it's only forty-year mortgages and an embracing of debt that sustain the unsustainable. Egged on by real estate marketing machines and reassured by economists paid by our largest lenders, we cling to the absurd belief that paying too much for something is okay. There will always be a greater fool willing to pay more.

Contrary to what you've been told, it was not subprime mortgages—giving loans to unworthy borrowers—that caused the American housing crisis and came to precipitate a global recession. That was but a symptom. The disease was a rush into real estate following the shock of 9/11, thanks to the flood of cheap money which washed over us in its wake. History will show that was a disastrous policy, leading so many into the worst mistake of their lives. It will also confirm there was no wall separating Calgary or Montreal or Regina from the rest of the world.

For many Canadians, unlike our Southern friends, there's still time to avoid what's coming. But taking action will require the ability to see that common wisdom is wrong, your neighbours are gamblers, the media message is distorted and misleading, and *Flip This House* is real estate pornography.

—Garth Turner

CHAPTER ONE

DEWEY-EYED IN HOME DEPOT

ONE DAY NOT LONG AGO, a two-storey half house in the dodgy East York section of Toronto changed hands for $463,000. Two bathrooms, three bedrooms and an 18-foot-wide lot.

Twenty-six Leroy Avenue hit the market just ten days earlier, asking $359,000. The owners received multiple offers, then sold it for a $104,000 premium, or a third more than they figured. Not bad. They'd bought the old brick structure three years earlier, for $326,000. In turn, they took it over from folks who snagged it for $151,500.

"It appealed to a number of buyers because it showed beautifully," agent Christina Paisley said of the property, "and the majority of the home was updated. It's still affordable to first-time buyers."

It is?

With 25 per cent down, the new buyers needed $115,000 in cash, then a mortgage of $348,000, with monthly and property tax payments of $2,821. To meet normal qualifications, they'd require an annual income of $101,556. But the median family income in Toronto is $54,399. And things are not normal.

"East York," explained agent Paisley in a *National Post* article, "is a hot neighbourhood."

What's wrong with this picture? What was the house worth? Was the selling price the same as the market value, or the appraised value? Did the buyers panic and pay an absurd premium in the emotion of a bidding war, scratching out numbers on an offer as they sat in a realtor's car idling at the curb?

How could the agent promote this property as ideally suited to first-time buyers, when it took twice the median income to carry it, and a down payment three times the average disposable annual income to buy it? Was that a blatant untruth? Did her employer, the largest real estate firm in Canada, rake her for misrepresentation? Or did the comments slip within the popular myth that real estate, whatever it costs, whatever the burden of ownership and wherever the economy leads, is a peerless investment? Were the new owners of twenty-six Leroy as wise as the sellers? Or the greater fools?

ABOUT THE SAME TIME, a five hour plane ride southwest, Rosa and Alex Lejis were telling the *Napa Valley Register* about their house in Manteca, a suburban beauty for which they paid $500,000 two years earlier. Like millions of Americans and Canadians, they were caught up in the dizzying ascent of real estate which hit North America following 9/11. As in Toronto and Calgary and Vancouver, real estate values in California climbed steadily, meaning any amount of mortgage debt was soon being eased by swelling, throbbing equity.

But, they didn't see the train headed their way. Rising interest rates, dwindling numbers of buyers and unsustainable prices combined in cruel fashion. As the value of homes rose, the number of people who could afford them declined. And when their adjustable rate mortgage came due for refinancing, monthly payments jumped from $3,200 to $4,000.

They decided to sell. But there were no buyers. After months of trying to get out, they gave up and surrendered the home to foreclosure. The half-million dollar house went on the market as a power of sale property, for $299,000. Still no buyers.

"We counted on being able to refinance," Rosa said. The size of the debt did not matter. The cost of the debt did.

As it turned out, this was one of 1,932 foreclosures in their area the first nine months of 2007. "Too many new houses. Too many investors. Too many exotic loans. They created a lethal mix," the local paper analyzed, "that caused the northern San Joaquin Valley's housing market to soar, then crash into a painful collage of foreclosures, unsold homes and financial woes."

What's wrong with this picture? Is the asking price of this house—4 per cent less than Rosa and Alex paid twenty-one months earlier—the market value, or the real value, or a bargain of historic significance? Did the owners panic and walk away at the worst possible moment? Or were they canny to default on a mortgage worth more than the actual value of the home? Did they lose because no fool came along to buy the asset for which they'd clearly paid too much? Should they ever have purchased a home they could not really afford? Or been allowed to?

IN 2007, IT WAS the fastest growing town in Canada. The population of Milton, forty clicks west of Toronto, mushroomed by more than 70 per cent, swelled by a tidal wave of largely first-time buyers desperate to secure a 43-foot lot in a former farm field with a new house planted in it. After all, that was seven feet more dirt than the same money bought down the highway, in Mississauga. Besides, there were horse farms just fifteen minutes away.

So great was the demand that Mattamy Homes, the area's chief developer, erected a massive steel building housing a new home assembly line, turning out one finished dwelling, dining room chandelier included, every sixteen hours. Behind it were nine more on the line. Average price, around $430,000. What had been a moderately-bustling former farm town five years earlier, whose major industry was a prison, became one more patch in the endless quiltwork of suburban sprawl and Big Box stores hugging the 401 highway all the way back to Pearson Airport.

But as the newbies poured in, overflowing the presentation centre's parking lot on Sundays, the market enthusiasm was suddenly failing to flow upward. In fact, during 2007, local 905 real estate agents were stunned at the numbers showing up on their MLS summary sheets, and even more so at what was happening on the streets of Milton.

In an upscale rural subdivision of near-identical estate homes, a two-acre spread on a crescent sold late in the year for $715,000, less than it fetched thirty months earlier, and only after seven months on the market and four price reductions.

Eight houses down the street, a similar property had changed hands one year earlier for $1.2 million. In early 2008, the house and property right next door could be purchased for $500,000 less. But after nine months, no buyers. Suddenly, the million-dollar homebuyers awoke to the fact they'd likely paid half a million too much—money which at that moment, had vaporized.

A kilometre away, a newly-reconstructed house on an acreage, listed at $1.3 million, was repriced at 30 per cent less. No buyers. The same month, RE/MAX issued a forecast for real estate performance in 2008. Said spokesman Eldon Ash, "Clearly, economic prosperity has translated into increased housing sales and upward pressure on prices across the board. The country's economic engine fired on all cylinders throughout the year, despite dire conditions south of the border. As in 2007, inventory will be the major wildcard next year—the ultimate variable most expected to influence housing market conditions and performance. A return to tight market conditions could mean all bets are off as buyers are forced to compete, creating increased market pressure."

On the crescent, the bets were already over. The owners lost.

After eighteen years of creating wealth, real estate was set to erase it. The lingering question: would this be a correction, or a collapse?

IS REAL ESTATE WORTH only what someone will pay for it? And if that's the case, how can an "affordable" home for first-timers in Toronto sell for a price not affordable to over 80 per cent of the population? Are we courting disaster by continuing to concentrate our wealth in an over-valued asset destined to fall in value? Or is Canada's real estate market somehow unique in the world, protected from forces now sweeping other lands?

Maybe not. In Britain, for example, house prices fell in 2007 for the first time in several years while a bank, Northern Rock, suffered a run on deposits—unheard of in a century. Pressure mounted on the Bank of England to cut interest rates in a bid to rescue a decade-long housing boom. Consumer credit was drying up, making it harder for families to shoulder the record debts run up because of a tripling of real estate prices since 1997. According to a 2007 Goldman Sachs report, tough, global growth was grinding to a halt. Of thirty-eight countries surveyed by the forecasting firm, twenty-six were forecast to slow in 2008. America, the catalyst, teetered on the brink of recession.

By early 2008, the global credit crisis was also hitting Canadian borrowers and homeowners. Quietly, all major banks cut the discount they offered customers on mortgages, as their profits were bombed with losses in the American market. Canadians negotiating variable rate loans found themselves paying a higher rate than just months earlier, while fixed-rate loans also jumped, raising monthly mortgage payments and reducing real estate affordability.

In late 2007, former American central banker Alan Greenspan, the man in charge of rescuing the US economy after the shock of 9/11, fended off sharp criticism that his own actions helped create a housing crisis. "Markets are becoming aware of the fact that the decline in house prices is not stopping," he said. "I have no particular regrets. The housing bubble is not a reflection of what we did, as it is a global phenomenon."

As a global credit crunch spread into 2008, signs were growing that the American housing meltdown—the inevitable conclusion of the asset bubble Greenspan acknowledged—might be heading south. Conditions, ironically, were made worse by the runaway Canadian dollar. What the federal government boasted as a "strong currency" actually weakened the economy dramatically. The move to parity with the American greenback, as Scotiabank economist Andrew Pyle put it, "basically means the time lag between when the U.S. hits a downturn or a steep slowdown, and when Canada hits a slowdown, has narrowed. I think the hit to Canada is going to be fairly quick."

To the south, foreclosures surpassed an all-time high in 2007 and the National Association of Realtors (NAR) reported existing home sales plunged for the year. The number of single-family homes changing hands hit the lowest level in twenty-five years; average prices eroded for the first time since records started to be kept four decades ago; and NAR economist Lawrence Yun said it was likely the first real year-over-year dive for home prices "since the Great Depression" of the 1930s.

"It looks grim," said consumer credit analyst John Litt in Houston, Texas. With more than two million unsold resale homes in the States and unsold inventories of new homes exploding as buyers cancelled contracts; with 20,000 empty homes in Phoenix alone; with home prices falling in virtually every American market (Miami, San Diego and Detroit all down by 13 per cent); with Goldman Sachs warning of a "vicious cycle" in housing likely to lead to a dramatic collapse in mortgage lending; with new home sales in 2007 plunging by 40 per cent and the average price off 11 per cent overall—and by 50 per cent on homes over $400,000; and with experts estimating house values would crash 25 per cent or more before finding bottom, the future looked obvious to some.

"The housing recovery is absolutely going to be measured in years, not in months," said New Jersey mortgage analyst Sue Woodward. Sales of existing homes in the autumn of 2007 dropped to the lowest point since 1999—when local stats started to be recorded. Despite massive price cuts and sellers offering to pay closing costs, while throwing in furniture and cars, unsold inventory continued to swell to record levels.

While mortgages in Canada became harder to get, and more expensive when you did, the Canadian dollar was silently vaporizing hundreds of thousands of manufacturing jobs, making exports prohibitively expensive, flooding the country with cheap imports, many from China, and ambushed retailers as shoppers—egged on by the federal minister of finance—demanded cheap, US-style prices, and clogged the border. The inevitable result was a looming economic slowdown, a drop in disposable income, rising unemployment, higher loan and mortgage costs, and a body blow to the service sector, which accounts for seven of every ten jobs.

Meanwhile, Canadians were being told real estate is solid, golden, stable. The Re/Max Housing Market Outlook 2008, for example, predicted better economic prospects for the country and price "appreciation ranging from 1 to 7 per cent" in all eighteen markets surveyed.

"There is no bubble," continued Barbara Lawlor, of Toronto-based Baker Real Estate, which specializes in condo sales. "We are not experiencing the same economic underpinnings today," as during the 1980s, which preceded a real estate downturn. What's different this time is low inflation, strong immigration and "our peaceful democratic society," she told The Globe and Mail.

In Calgary, 2008's incoming real estate board president, Ed Jensen, had two words, when asked for advice to buyers: "Buy now." Despite the fact that the average home in Calgary had catapulted $72,000 higher in price, and the average condo was $53,000 more expensive. Jensen said, "From the buying perspective, there's no question in my mind that 2008 is going to be an excellent year and I believe that the prices will increase. So, buy now while there's selection."

Calgarians, as it turned out, ponied up $13.3 billion to buy houses in 2007, while Canadians in general spent a stunning $118 billion on homes, the greatest amount of money ever, and a breathtaking 19.6 per cent more than in the previous year. "The statistics show just how dynamic the Canadian housing market was in virtually all parts of the country," boasted Canadian Real Estate Association (CREA) president Ann Bosley. "The record sales activity also shows it remains a very affordable real estate market."

But how could that be? The average house price in Canada that year was $326,055. With the average downpayment (15 per cent), that would require more than $50,000 upon closing and an annual income of more than $70,000 to carry. But that was more than the average family earned.

Despite the obvious, the industry hype is non-stop. "Momentum for sales activity remains strong, and sales are forecast to reach their second-highest levels on record this year," CREA economist Gregory Klump said in 2008. "Additional interest rate cuts this year will keep resale housing market activity on a strong footing and prices will continue to rise but at a slower pace."

Sentiment like this helped create a hyped-up, days-long lineup of buyers in late 2007 for luxury condos to be built in mid-town Toronto. Undoubtedly, it helped the sellers of twenty-six Leroy Ave. to a hundred thousand dollar windfall, and the purchasers to swallow an extra $104,000 in debt. It helped delude streets of young, mortgaged homeowners in Milton their assembly-line homes and forty feet of soil could only appreciate in value. They might suddenly have forty-year mortgages and crippling monthly payments. But, how could they lose?

At that moment, house prices were dropping in 54 of 150 American cities. The housing slump that began in 2006 was entering its third, and perhaps most gruesome year.

Books and TV shows cater to housing mania

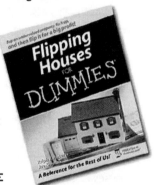

CANADIAN FAMILIES HAVE

more than 80 per cent of their net worth in residential real estate, according to bank surveys. Concurrently, Statistics Canada says the national savings rate is zero. Fully half of all adults have no retirement savings.

Real estate investing, and the hope of quick profits surged into the media mainstream. When everybody's doing it, time to exit?
— *Flipping Houses for Dummies*, by Ralph Roberts, Joe Kraynak

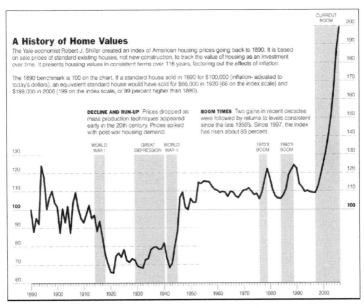

A History of Home Values

The Yale economist Robert J. Shiller created an index of American housing prices going back to 1890. It is based on sale prices of standard existing houses, not new construction, to track the value of housing as an investment over time. It presents housing values in consistent terms over 116 years, factoring out the effects of inflation.

The 1890 benchmark is 100 on the chart. If a standard house sold in 1890 for $100,000 (inflation- adjusted to today's dollars), an equivalent standard house would have sold for $66,000 in 1920 (66 on the index scale) and $199,000 in 2006 (199 on the index scale, or 99 percent higher than 1890).

DECLINE AND RUN-UP Prices dropped as mass production techniques appeared early in the 20th century. Prices spiked with post-war housing demand.

BOOM TIMES Two gains in recent decades were followed by returns to levels consistent since the late 1950's. Since 1997, the index has risen about 83 percent.

Yale economist and author Robert Shiller created this index of American housing prices going back to 1890, based on the value of resale homes, to gauge real estate as an investment. Factoring out inflation, it compares housing values over 116 years. It's not hard to see the recent boom took on a bubble status.

— *Irrational Exuberance*, 2nd edition, 2006, by Robert Shiller

Mortgage debt and household consumer debt are at historic highs. At the same time, seven in ten of us have no pension plans other than the meagre allowance offered by CPP. Clearly, we have put our faith, and our futures, into houses. We've invested, of course. But have we also gambled?

No wonder there's been a fetish for bricks and mortar. For all the time most Canadians have been alive, residential real estate's been a stellar performer—keeping pace with, or exceeding, inflation. Housing has proved to be a worthwhile long-term storehouse of wealth, and has formed the cornerstone of personal financial planning. True, values have sometimes taken a dive—historically during times of conflict or economic downturn—but they've always rebounded, since this is a commodity unlike no other.

Real estate is affected by the same forces which move the price of gold, wheat and uranium, like supply and demand, and inflation.

But it's also a uniquely human product, fabricated by our own hands and supplying something we all require—shelter.

Over time, though, its value has become unhinged from the service it provides, and housing has become an emotional and financial object of desire. Judging by the number of get-rich-quick real estate books and reality real estate shows there are on North American TV, we've become obsessed. Judging by prices, at least until recently, the obsession has paid off.

But can an asset class rise in value forever? Investors in gold bullion thought so in the late 1970s, when they bought the metal at a price which would not be seen again for almost thirty years—in early 2008, in the wake of the American real estate collapse and growing fears of recession. The same fate awaited those who put their life savings into tulips in 1636, when a single bulb could fetch as much as the modern equivalent of $40,000. It was an orgy of speculation which the Dutch government tried in vain to stop. (It failed, the bubble burst, and economic depression in the Netherlands ensued.) Ditto for those who bought into money-losing dot-com companies in 2000 at prices which doubled every two months for stock in companies without profits. For most of us, all booms, it seems, turn out badly.

Another characteristic of booms is this: The common wisdom during one is, "this time it will be different." Despite what later appears to be insurmountable and irrefutable evidence of excess and over-valuations, investors chasing a hot commodity are blinded to the inevitable consequences of their actions. They crash. They burn. They never learn.

House prices, Japan, US, UK, Australia

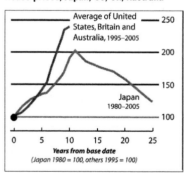

Average of United States, Britain and Australia, 1995–2005

Japan 1980–2005

250
200
150
100

0   5   10   15   20   25
Years from base date
(Japan 1980 = 100, others 1995 = 100)

Before the bubble burst in late 2005, the US housing market tracked that of several Western nations and, ominously, of Japan. Investors there waited 16 years for prices to start recovering.

— *The Economist* magazine, June 16, 2005

Of course, real estate bubbles are not new. And so far, they've all ended up pretty much the same way. Japan in the 1980s was a great example, with prices hitting a historic high before crashing back to earth with such force that the Bank of Japan reduced interest rates to zero to try and keep the economy afloat. It has taken the better part of twenty years for residential real estate prices to recover.

The chart here (Japan Nationwide Land Prices) gives another representation of that experience, which has found wide Internet circulation among crestfallen American homeowners. Many of them look at the misfortune of others who have gone before, and wonder how they could have missed so many warning signs.

What makes real estate decline in value? Here are the eight factors I believe are irrepressible. When any one of these materializes, real estate becomes less desirable. When a few of them combine, housing takes a hit.

Where does the Canadian real estate sit now?

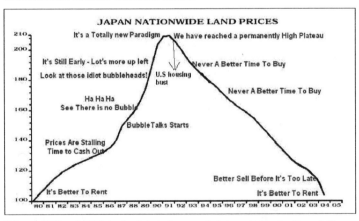

Between 1980 and 2005, land values in Japan exploded, peaked and collapsed. The experience is now being used as a template for a classic real estate investment bubble. Many American observers believe US real estate is on a similar course. Meanwhile, could the Canadian market be hovering at the 'new Paradigm' stage?

— globaleconomicanalysis blog

Real estate markets inevitably fall...
1. When supply and demand get out of whack.
2. When prices rise so far, so fast, the average family can't afford the average home.
3. When job loss or economic downturn robs buyers of the confidence needed to take on mortgage debt.
4. When prices start to fall and people realize they can buy more for less if they simply wait.
5. When an aging population means house-rich and cash-poor people, like today's baby boomers, are suddenly desperate to sell.
6. When the cost of money rises, making credit expensive and houses unaffordable.
7. When a boom is not based on rising personal incomes and job growth, but rather on speculation. The boom is then a bubble.
8. When the pendulum of investor greed swings too far in one direction, and inevitably swings back, triggering panic selling.

Today, every one of those factors is at play, at the same time. Not for at least an entire generation, therefore, has real estate in

Calgary and Vancouver also in bubble territory?

Residential real estate values in Vancouver (left) and Calgary (right) have about doubled in value since the pivotal events of 9/11, and the subsequent collapse in borrowing costs.

— Real Estate Board of Greater Vancouver, Calgary Real Estate Board

Canada been so at risk, nor have we had an example so close—just south of the border—of what is to come. And never have we had so much to lose.

House prices in both Calgary and Vancouver have roughly doubled since 9/11. In Toronto, values are higher by about 60 per cent. Sales overall are stable. But the numbers sometimes mislead.

In the 905 belt surrounding Toronto—as the rural Milton example exemplified—sales of homes priced over $700,000 all but collapsed in the second half of 2007, while new home buyers continued to flood in, since 5 per cent down payments and newly-introduced forty-year mortgages masked affordability erosion. In fact, "official" market statistics, gathered, interpreted and published by local real estate boards usually fail to identify price trends and sub-market movements which can have great significance.

In this instance, the disappearance of high-end sales underscored a fear among older, wealthier, experienced buyers that the economy was wobbly and the market grossly over-valued. On the other hand, young couples with no previous buying experience—and little to lose—continued to believe the industry-fed storyline that real estate can only appreciate. Realtors might be able to ignore the facts on high-end buyers, but if declining prices reduce new homebuyers' equity to zero, or bring house values below mortgage amounts, it will be an entirely different story.

But, then, how bad could it possibly get?

After all, real estate values have been on a steady upward trajectory in Canada since the bottom of the last downturn, in the early 1990s. While many people expect a boom market to moderate in the next few years, hardly anyone seriously contemplates a crash.

After all, the industry has been categoric and unwavering in its analysis of housing conditions. Here is the assessment Royal LePage president and CEO Phil Soper made in late autumn of 2007:

"Much like the Canadian dollar, the Canadian housing market is charting its own course, quite independent from the United States and its currency and housing climate. The strength of the Canadian dollar, and the fact that the country is adjusting well to its value, will continue to keep interest rates at their existing low-to-moderate levels, boding well for buyers looking to enter the market. From coast-to-coast, the country's rich commodity markets have had tremendous impact on local economies, and there is no indication this will change anytime soon."

Accompanying that was a corporate report showing two-storey house prices were up year-over-year by 24 per cent in Boucherville, 18 per cent in north Toronto, 65 per cent in Saskatoon, 23 per cent in Edmonton and 14 per cent in Vancouver.

The unmistakable message: This is not America. Our currency is a symbol of our strength. Time to buy real estate.

Unmentioned, of course, was the actual impact the high dollar was having on the country. The manufacturing sector lost almost 90,000 jobs in 2007, and was bracing for a spate of factory and mill closures in the months to come. Ignored was the fact that record house prices had already condemned most first-time buyers to a staggering load of mortgage debt, and that banks were actively tightening credit. And unreported was the fact that our biggest trading partner, most important customer and dominant economy in the Western world was inexorably on the slide. Canadian family income was stuck in the mud, energy costs were escalating, high value-added jobs being exported and the dollar rendering the country uncompetitive.

Added Mr. Soper:

"Despite the rising house prices across the country, recent Statscan reports cite that the home ownership rate stands at its highest on record. With the combination of the cost of borrowing money remaining relatively low, the availability of longer mortgage amortization periods, and the fact that Canada's population continues to grow, it is no surprise that more and more people are entering the real estate market."

Was this responsible corporate commentary? Or industry shilling?

More importantly to all those people Phil Soper was encouraging to buy into the market at that moment was this: could the unthinkable actually take place here? Truth be told, it was only a couple of years ago that people in places like Minneapolis and St. Paul were feeling pretty confident about their own financial futures.

But as Royal LePage in Toronto was pumping the housing market, auctioneers in Minneapolis were dumping it.

More than 300 homes on auction block

Want to purchase a house for half its price? More than 300 foreclosed homes across Minnesota will be auctioned this weekend. "It's a sign of the times" and just a fraction of the fallout from the subprime mortgage meltdown.

In the largest sell-off of its kind in Minnesota, more than 300 foreclosed homes across the state will go on the auction block this weekend.

The mass two-day sale at the Minneapolis Convention Center will unload one-bedroom condos, tiny ramblers, stately gabled Victorians and even sprawling suburban houses to the highest bidders.

Repossessed after their owners didn't make payments, the properties are victims of a real estate market devastated by the subprime mortgage meltdown.

Minnesota Association of Realtors vice president Chris Galler said it's the biggest auction he's seen in his two decades in the business. Auctions normally dispose of a half-dozen to a dozen homes. "It's a sign of the times," Galler said. For Irvine, Calif.-based Real Estate Disposition Corp., the boom in foreclosures has meant opportunity. The company has crisscrossed the country auctioning as many as 600 repossessed homes at a time. The company has stopped in about 10 cities this year and has five more scheduled after Minneapolis.

The properties listed offer some enticing potential bargains. At a starting bid of a mere $9,000, someone could pick up a 1,072-square-foot cheery home with red shutters, hardwood floors and 1907-vintage woodwork on Upton Avenue in north Minneapolis. It was once valued at $47,900.

Across the river in southeast Minneapolis, a 1,574-square-foot unit 14 floors up in the La Rive condominiums is vacant and awaiting a new owner. It has shell-shaped his-and-her bathroom sinks, updated appliances and sweeping views of the historic riverfront. Previous valuation: $515,000. Starting bid: $229,000.

Looking for a suburban retreat? A 1978 home in Shakopee offers three bedrooms, three baths and a 1-acre lot with 150 feet of shoreline on O'Dowd Lake. Previous valuation: $710,000. Starting bid: $229,000.

Real Estate Disposition Corp. got its start with property auctions in the 1990s. Properties auctioned that decade originated with developers, and unlike this year's auctions, not from homeowners who defaulted on mortgage payments.

The number of houses being auctioned today and Sunday isn't even a notable fraction of the number of foreclosed homes in the state. Last month, foreclosures in Minnesota were up 183 percent from a year ago, to 1,510. The rate was one filing for every 1,491 households.

— *Minneapolis Star Tribune*, October 20, 2007

Worse news, however, was on the way. According to Scotiabank's senior economist, Carlos Gomes, a third of all mortgages taken out in the States between 2004 and 2006 had adjustable rates. Most of them offered bargain-basement rates of interest for the first two or three years which are then reset. Gomes estimated four million such mortgages would be reset at higher rates during 2008, with a substantial economic impact, something that obviously was keeping the American president awake at night.

The magnitude of the problem was reflected in the sweep of the response. As 2007 drew to a close, George Bush agreed to an emergency rescue plan engineered by the U.S. Treasury Department and the mortgage industry, aimed at preventing an avalanche of new home foreclosures. Washington told lenders it expected them to freeze for five years the "teaser" rates they had extended to homebuyers with new mortgages. Loans originated between the first days of 2005 and the summer of 2007, coming up for reset between January 2008 and the summer of 2010 would be eligible, meaning struggling homeowners would continue to struggle—but not be forced from their homes.

As many was 1.2 million owners were potentially affected, but even this desperate and unprecedented move was hailed as a recipe for disaster. Worse, maybe, a mere finger in the dike of real estate collapse.

"Freezing adjustable mortgages at teaser rates will only push the problem to the next president," was how a business professor in Maryland, Peter Morici, put it. At the same time, Standard & Poor's Corp. The Wall Street analysts and bond raters said the plan would have a devastating impact on bondholders, making them much more exposed, while investment and market guru Dennis Gartman said Bush had broken the bond between borrower and lender and would lead to a "tsunami-like" wave of legal action. After all, for every mortgage on one side, there are investors on the other. Changing the terms on mortgages means gouging people who were counting on that interest as income. As a Bloomberg business news commentary put it, "Moody's Investors Services is preparing the biggest credit rating cuts since subprime mortgages contaminated the bond market, foreshadowing losses for investments that pay Florida teachers and money market funds."

In fact, nobody was sounding too confident about the coming years. "This is not a silver bullet," Treasury Secretary Henry Paulson told reporters as the announcement was made. "We face a difficult problem for which there is no perfect solution." Within days of that, the American central bank underscored the gravity of the situation, by again chopping its key lending rate a quarter point, reducing market mortgage rates. The irony here was large: It was cheap money that bred the subprime crisis which now threatened to topple the entire American housing market and plunge the country into a job-sucking recession.

This stab at rescuing the inevitable from collapse was repeated at the end of January 2008, as global stock markets plunged amid news US real estate would continue to topple. Washington responded in dramatic fashion, passing an emergency bailout package which would send every adult American a cheque for $600, while making it easier for people to borrow "jumbo" mortgages—those above $417,000. The Fed this time dropped rates a stunning three-quarters of a point and followed it up a week later with another half-point slash. And the best solution seemed to be...more cheap money.

Could the outcome be in doubt?

FLAWED AS IT MAY have been, the Bush bail-outs may have been one of the few options Washington had in the midst of the greatest personal finance and banking crisis since the 1930s. By saving over-burdened homeowners, the administration was actually more worried about the lenders than the loans. The post-9/11 American house of cards, built on the asset inflation of real estate, was in danger of toppling.

In a Tampa, Florida, suburb, two months earlier, Greg Armstrong said he had never seen anything like it before. Of the twenty-one houses which his Coldwell Banker office had sold in a month, a dozen had been foreclosed on by lenders after owners had walked.

Armstrong, president of the local real estate board, told the *Tampa Tribune*: "I've been in business for seventeen years, and I've never seen the bank be the number one seller. Lenders can afford to go much lower in price than homeowners can. The banks don't want all these homes, so they'll sell them for whatever they need to."

Of course, banks dumping houses just made the situation worse for everyone, them included. With each bargain-basement foreclosure sale, average prices in the neighbourhood dropped to a new lowest common denominator. Homeowners concluding they had to sell for financial reasons soon also realized they couldn't break even with prices plunging. In fact, even foreclosure was often ruled out as an option. Instead, many chose to simply go bankrupt—absolving themselves entirely of a mortgage debt worth more than the homes they'd bought.

Banks in the United States, like those here, want loans, not houses. In Florida, California, New York and elsewhere, some owners have just dropped off deeds at their local bank branches, often unaware they will be sued for the shortfall between the bargain-basement sale price and the face amount of their mortgage.

In this toxic real estate environment, Washington's desperate plan to stem foreclosures, defaults, bad loans and bankruptcies was clearly an attempt to buy time. If hundreds of thousands, or millions, of Americans could be kept in their houses, making payments, then the financial dominoes might not fall as quickly. Perhaps some time—a year or two—would stabilize the housing market, but only if the abandonment of homes could be halted.

Back to the suburbs of Tampa, and to what was once (two years ago) called "the perfect neighbourhood on the surface." In Thousand Oaks East, a home on a corner is where the local kids catch the school bus. It's abandoned now, so the remaining neighbours take turns cutting the grass so children don't have to stand in knee-high weeds.

In this enclave, 128 of 191 homes are for sale, or have been given up after six months on the market without a nibble. On one street there are six foreclosures. One has a sign saying "$60,000 under appraised value." But, no buyers.

By and large, the people who bought homes here at high prices, who plunked money down and took on big mortgage debt for which they qualified, did not do anything wrong. As with families in suburban Calgary, Toronto or Kelowna, they

What goes up: US house price index, 1990–2007

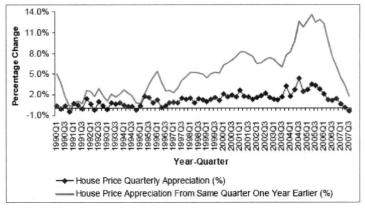

Over the course of almost two decades, American real estate prices appreciated in a fairly narrow range until rock-bottom interest rates clicked in, fuelling speculation and asset inflation. The bubble burst at the end of 2005—an event economists now say was inevitable.

— Office of Federal Housing Enterprise Oversight, Washington

believed in the future of real estate, in its seemingly endless ability to appreciate and grow equity. That appreciation was supposed to shrink the relative size of the debt and grow their wealth while they enjoyed a new home in an unblemished community.

How could they know the market would turn and prices erode, making the mortgage swell until it consumed every dollar of value that property once held? At first, the decision was whether or not to sell and move. Then it was whether to take a loss, or hang on until things got better. After that came the devastating realization they might have to walk, surrendering the house to foreclosure. Or worse, declare bankruptcy and lose all.

Through it all they asked "how could this happen?"

A better question may have been, how could it not?

BETWEEN CHRISTMAS OF 2006 and the end of 2007, average house prices in Toronto climbed by 11 per cent. In Vancouver they jumped 12.7 per cent and almost 9 per cent in Calgary (down from a 36 per cent increase in the previous year).

In all three cities, average prices hit an all-time high of $395,000, $540,000 and $410,000 respectively. In Vancouver, the average detached home sold for more than $700,000 and the average condo for $375,000.

In other words, in these three major urban areas, it took more money to buy the average home than the average family had, or could qualify to borrow. To bridge the gap, growing numbers of new buyers raided their RRSPS, increased mortgage debt, borrowed from family members or extended their mortgage amortizations, thereby swelling the amount to be repaid.

Record prices. Record debt. Longer repayment. Little down. Less equity. And still, the panic to purchase continued unabated.

Savio and Hillary Rodrigues are both in their 30. In late 2006 they decided to buy a home in Toronto. Their budget: $450,000, more than fifty thousand dollars above the average house price.

The first home they put an offer on was in Greektown. Theirs was one of sixteen offers the owners received, and they lost to a couple who put down an additional $60,000 over the asking price. Finally, after losing in five more bidding wars, the young, first-time buyers found a renovated two-storey resale home in the High Park area, and snagged it by offering $20,000 more than the seller—who was moving out of the country and wanted a quick sale—was looking for.

So, they finally had their home—for $700,000, or $350,000 more than they planned on spending.

As Savio, a product manager with IBM, told the *Toronto Star*, "It really didn't hit us until we told Hillary's parents, who are from Bowmanville and their eyes kind of widened. Her dad just said, 'you could by four homes in Bowmanville for that money.'"

Savio and Hillary justify their extravagance by pointing to the investment track record of residential real estate. The last time it declined in value was when they were both in high school. And if they paid a little too much, well, how bad could it get? It would just take a little longer for them to actually be making money, even though the mortgage was more than $300,000 bigger than they'd planned on.

Right?

DESPITE WASHINGTON'S late-2007 stab at stemming the market decline and braking the slowdown in the American economy, few people were hopeful as 2008 dawned. More and more homeowners continued to be pushed into foreclosure, helping to force overall real estate values lower, and leading to more market-destroying events like the Minneapolis auction.

After all, cheap money had been the gasoline fuelling the market flames, but it did not start the fire. That was greed. "It's not the mortgage that's the problem," a Los Angeles economist said of Bush's plan. It's that "homeowners paid too much for their homes in a soaring market, and are now facing the dire consequences."

Ironically, real estate-crazed Canadians are now seen as one of the few bright spots in the American housing market. With the loonie near par, and US house prices decimated, many Canucks are taking the plunge where local buyers fear to tread. In Washington State, local Whatcom Country agent Mike Kent says, "With Vancouver-area home prices so high right now, we look like a bargain in comparison."

In Florida, where prices dropped by as much as a third in a year, Canadians are being courted aggressively by realtors whose local phone lines were dead months ago. A Naples golf course condo has slid in price from $350,000 to less than $230,000. And in Arizona, builders like Farnsworth Developments are

Snapshot of a housing market gone mad?

The smallest house in Toronto, built on a former driveway, was on the market in late 2007. Nine feet wide, asking $173,000. Its previous sale was six months earlier, at $135,000.

offering upgrades to new homes worth $30,000, in addition to lower prices.

Compared to Canada, housing is cheap, absurdly so. But what if the American experience is a foretelling of ours? What if, contrary to what Royal LePage boss Soper told the media, the Canadian housing market is not charting its own course, but merely lagging it? Are there solid reasons why our market should soar, when theirs crashes? Are we immune to a real estate correction after a decade of gains? Are Canadian houses going to increase in value forever?

Of course not. But that's exactly the shaky premise upon which millions of current homeowners have taken action and rolled the dice. Are you one?

ONE ESTIMATE PUTS at 40 per cent the number of all new jobs created in California in the past five years which were real estate-related. This was bizarre and unsustainable, the creation of a real estate bubble fed, in part, by what the industry calls "innovative" mortgage lending practices.

In the third quarter of 2007, 72,751 California homeowners walked away from their homes, an increase in foreclosures of 166 per cent from the same period a year earlier, and setting a new record. The impact? "We know now, in emerging detail, that a lot of these loans shouldn't have been made. The issue is whether the real estate market and the economy will digest these over the next year or two, or if housing market distress will bring the economy to its knees," said Marshall Prentice, of DataQuick Information Systems.

California defaults soared 166 per cent in late 2007

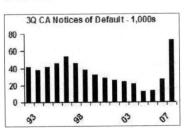

3Q CA Notices of Default - 1,000s

More than 72,000 homeowners in California walked away from their properties in the third quarter of 2007 alone. More than a million Americans have lost their homes in the market collapse.
— California Association of Realtors

In Detroit, it's a similar story. By the end of 2007, there were seven hundred homes for sale in Motor City's swankiest neighbourhoods in Grosse Pointe, twice as many as in 2005. Prices for the most expensive homes were dropping by about $100,000 each month.

Across the United States, the supply of foreclosed homes suddenly hit 45 per cent of all existing home sales, adding about four months' supply to existing homes, and extending the agony of those sellers desperate to get out of mortgage debt which had come to entrap them.

Defenders of the Canadian housing market—industry insiders and bank economists—say the same meltdown could not happen in this country, because of stricter lending criteria, tighter mortgage granting practices and risk-averse banks which dominate the market. But, that's a myth.

NO MONEY IS ALSO NO PROBLEM IN CANADA.

Canada's real estate bubble has been fed by the same orgy of debt which created the American disaster, now eating up the wealth of millions of homeowners. It is a complete fabrication that lenders here have not engaged in the same cavalier, loan-at-any-cost practices, as competition trumped caution. Since the autumn of 2006, for example, even borrowers at the country's big banks have not needed any actual money to buy a house, with the advent of no-money-down mortgages.

In fact, the country's once-staid, conservative banks have been at the forefront of feeding a real estate frenzy by shoving on piles of new debt. In the summer of 2006, for example, RBC's assistant chief economist, Derek Holt, published a paper titled, *Three Cheers for Mortgage Innovation!* Enthused economist Holt, "The mortgage market of the future will likely be thoroughly unrecognizable by today's standards. Furthermore, the structure of the economy-wide household balance sheet could become thoroughly transformed with higher debt-to-income ratios and higher leverage (or debt-to-assets) made possible through a healthy, logical product mix shift without compromising debt serviceability."

In other words (and as you would expect), the bank clearly dreams of a day when Canadians owe more, not less, in terms of both their incomes and the value of their homes. And that day is closer than ever.

For decades, we've been able to buy houses with just 5 per cent down, taking on 95 per cent financing, and yet even that low bar has been knocked down as home ownership comes to be seen as a right, and no longer a privilege. Our bankers and mortgage brokers have been only too happy to quietly usher in a suite of loans which rival most offerings in the debt-ravaged United States, from zero down financing to loans that provide 103 per cent or more of the price of a piece of real estate.

Derek Holt's paper touched on four of them. Interest-only mortgages allow purchasers to drop monthly payments for an initial period of time by paying back absolutely none of the outstanding principle. When normal debt repayment kicks in, payments jump. But by then, you are the happy owner of a big mortgage.

Subprime loans have also been available in Canada for the past few years, championed by companies like Toronto's Exceed Mortgage. These are designed for people who normally would never qualify for loans, because they have lousy credit, insecure employment or a history of going broke. "To call the Canadian experience a true sub-prime market," says Holt, "is a bit of a misnomer, near-prime would be a better characterization. This is because, unlike other countries, the Canadian sub-prime market is so far targeting individuals who have just slightly below-normal credit quality characteristics." That still means, without such a mortgage "innovation" they wouldn't get one.

Then there's the forty-year mortgage, which swept the marketplace in mere months after being introduced in 2007. By lengthening the typical amortization (the length of time until the mortgage is repaid) from twenty-five years to forty, monthly

Canadians, like Americans, give up saving

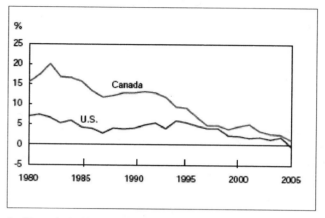

Families on both sides of the border have given up saving in favour of spending. Household incomes have stagnated, debt has swollen and the savings rate hit zero. Storm warning.

— Statistics Canada

payments drop substantially, while the total repayment costs of the loan skyrocket. But while it creates almost a life time indebtedness, a new attitude towards debt among young borrowers—who never envision a day when they own a mortgage-free house—makes it completely acceptable. In fact, banker friends tell me fifty-year "ams" will soon be the norm.

Hybrid mortgage products are also popping up routinely, giving borrowers the option of combining fixed and variable rate terms, along with blending mortgages and home equity loans. Coming out of that soon could be US-style "accordion mortgages," which keep monthly payments steady but expand or contract (without limit) the size of the debt to be repaid and the length of indebtedness, based on changing interest rates and the ability of the borrower to pay.

Of course, add to that the "Free Down Payment" loan which Scotiabank innovated, and which actually provides the 5 per cent down payment. TD Canada Trust's competing product asks new homebuyers to come up with only the closing costs—typically 2 per cent of the house value. Broker Mortgage

Intelligence offers 100 per cent financing and a 5 per cent cash-back feature. Broker BC Mortgage Loans will also give 100 per cent financing, but insists that "your credit report must be in good standing and you must have a good credit score with no bankruptcy in the past seven years." And how about a job? "Good steady employment," the company says, "and solid financial income will definitely help."

In launching its no-money-down mortgage, Scotiabank managing director of mortgages, Charles Lambert said, "We did some research and a number of people make a good living and wanted to get into the (real estate) market but had trouble coming up with the down payment." Solution? No down payment.

To his credit, bank economist Derek Holt does acknowledge the pivotal part debt-dealing banks may be playing in inflating the real estate bubble. "There is already evidence that financial innovation has played a role in supporting housing market activity for longer than many had anticipated," he says.

And it's hard to imagine he is not right. No real estate boom market can exist without debt. And it is the availability of cheap, easy credit, combined with an appetite for debt on the part of buyers, which helps turn a boom into a bubble. At the same time, providing financing to people without money, who haven't been able to save anything, who may have jobs but also have lots of other debt, with questionable credit ratings, or who qualify because they have a pulse, seems a certain way to ensure the bubble will eventually burst. Meanwhile, a sea of easy-to-grab mortgage money means more buyers, many of them flippers and speculators, enter the market, increasing demand and adding to the upward pressure on prices.

The inevitable conclusion is that the current Canadian real estate market is floating on a sea of unrepayable, and perhaps unserviceable, debt. In my community, there are thousands of new homebuyers who, at best, have purchased with 5 per cent down, while untold numbers of others are clients of TD, Scotia or other lenders who loaned them all the money they needed. In most cases, they are leveraged to the max, borrowing the greatest amount they qualified for, and living hand-to-mouth, while they feed the house.

That means, for them at least, the Canadian middle-class dream consists of a new house, a new minivan, a new baby, no savings, no disposable income and, if the housing market flatlines, no prospects. In fact, without steady, year-over-year real estate appreciation, they slide inexorably backwards—coughing up mortgage, utility and property tax payments which would be far less than the rental rate on the same home. In the case of a real estate market decline, even a modest one, those with some equity end up with none, and those who bought with nothing down suddenly owe more money than their homes are worth. So, why keep on owning them?

And how is this scenario—close at hand, I'd say—different from the mess that's destroyed the US real estate market? After all, without the first-time buyers who aspire to move up, any market runs out of fuel. The irony is that by dropping the lending bar and showering money on people with no savings and pre-existing debt, Canadian lenders have created the conditions under which we are ripe to import the American nightmare.

Remember, the US trouble started at the bottom of the market, not the top. In California, for example, of the tens of thousands of homeowners defaulting on their mortgages, and giving up their homes in the autumn of 2007, the average mortgage was $344,000—about what new buyers in suburban Toronto carry. At the time they quit their homes, they missed an average of five payments, and were $10,914 behind.

And while a little less than $11,000 does not sound like a lot of money, it is enough to create billions of dollars in equity losses for every homeowner as the defaults ultimately crash all market activity and deflate prices.

Also misleading is the myth that US real estate melted because unqualified people bought houses with loans they did not deserve. Instead, it crashed because middle-class Americans gorged on houses they could not have afforded if mortgages had not been discounted and downpayments ignored.

A *Wall Street Journal* analysis of more than $2.5 trillion in subprime mortgages found that in the peak year—2005—more than half of all these loans with cheap teaser rates were taken out by borrowers with relatively high credit ratings. "The surprisingly high number of subprime loans among more credit-worthy borrowers shows how far such mortgages spread into the economy—including middle-class and wealthy communities, where they once were scarce," the study concluded. "They also affirm that thousands of borrowers took out loans, perhaps foolishly, with little or no documentation, or no down payment, or without the income to qualify for a conventional loan of the size they wanted."

Too much house. Too much debt. Too few controls. And every day of every week in every major city in Canada, more young buyers, more speculators, more boomers buying trophy houses and cottages, more builders, more realtors, are all rolling the same dice.

Imagine new suburban streets with a half-dozen For Sale signs planted in each block. Interspersed are For Rent signs stuck in many windows. Everywhere you look, there are homes which are obviously no longer occupied, with weedy, unkempt front lawns and stacks of freebie community newspapers and mouldy flyers at the front doors.

Because the supply of homes has overwhelmed demand, asking prices keep declining. Each sale sets a new, lower standard for comparables on the street. The process robs every neighbour of equity and makes those who financed their way into a market they thought would rise forever, despair. It's a dreary scenario and, some would argue, a certainty in those areas where thousands of copycat homes sold quickly to thousands of similar families who were granted thousands of mortgages, which only made sense in a rising market.

Too often, sadly, those young buyers were more focused on granite counters and stone bathroom tiles than they were on the economic environment which could destroy the value of the homes they coveted. Throughout the second half of 2007, for example, hardly a day went by without more news of the mounting global credit crunch that had been spawned by the subprime mortgage crisis in the United States.

Worthless American mortgages which had been bundled into financial assets then sold around the world came quickly to threaten more than $30 billion held by Canadian banks and investors. By the end of 2007, the guy in charge of the Bank of Canada, David Dodge, was doing everything he could to underscore the crisis—sending out the clear signal this was going to hurt on the level of every suburban street corner in the country.

If this financial poison spreads further, he said, the consequences will be not be pretty. As he told the editorial board of the *National Post*, "If the whole market goes into a shambles, everybody gets affected, including Mr. and Mrs. Jones on Main Street. We have a collective interest in the whole thing not going into a shambles."

In other words, Dodge was telling every dewy-eyed set of homebuyers walking into Home Depot that losses on exotic products like non-bank, asset-backed commercial paper could, which a housing meltdown in another country created, end up crunching mortgages in Canada, restricting credit and precipitate a real estate disaster of our own. This was entirely consistent with his former American colleague, the globally-respected Alan Greenspan, who had already said simply that real estate was a "bubble."

Two years from now, we may look back on this and wonder how we missed the warning signals. Too many homes, developed too quickly into communities with no history, populated by inexperienced and over-financed owners with virtually no equity or stake in the community, and no reason to stay when the tide turned. A real estate industry so intoxicated with boom market conditions that it threw every resource into keeping the party going, and in the process betrayed the naïve trust of a generation of buyers. Lenders, including some of our largest and oldest banks, who abandoned caution and prudence, qualifying the unqualified and setting up to fail unworthy borrowers. Sellers, whose greed was sharpened and augmented by years of double-digit returns for a commodity—shelter—they needed, anyway. And buyers who bought on panic and allowed themselves to be the casualties of bidding wars and unrealistic expectations.

How could a smart, complex society, and especially the Google generation, have allowed itself such a false belief—that one commodity, real estate, would go up in value forever? Were we insane?

Or did we believe there'd always be a greater fool, than we?

CHAPTER TWO

THE WAKE-UP CALL

ONE MONDAY MORNING in dreary November 2007, Toronto agents Hersh Litvack (RE/MAX) and Anna Cass (Royal LePage), dragged some lawn chairs onto a downtown sidewalk and began what might come to be seen as the beginning of the end of the millennial Canadian real estate orgy.

For Mr. Litvak, it was a well-planned stunt. Three weeks earlier he began lining up young people who would take money in return for standing, sitting or lying in the cold, dark and rain. Then he booked a nearby hotel room for food and showers, and set his sites on One Bloor East.

By the time the new condo's sales centre doors opened eight days later, Litvak and Cass were standing at the start of a line of buyers that stretched back about a hundred people. They were all willing to buy up to three suites (the maximum), in a massive eighty-storey building, at prices averaging $850 for every single square foot. At that, a 700-square-foot bachelor pad was valued at almost $600,000, while the 80th floor penthouse was snapped up within a few days, for $25 million.

Said the developer, Bazis International of Kazakhstan (we're not making this up), "We believe prices of real estate are still undervalued compared to world cities. Yonge and Bloor is the most important corner in Toronto. We wanted to address it and do something for Toronto. The city has been tough, but supportive. We believe real estate prices have a long way to go." (Months later six Kazakh banks were caught in the US subprime meltdown, with credit downgrades and frozen loans.)

But, in which direction?

The scene was reminiscent of the last time buyers routinely lined up in all kinds of weather to buy unbuilt homes, in 1989 in Toronto, and 2005 in many American cities. During the housing booms in places like Mississauga in the eighties and Tampa and Las Vegas twenty years later, investors and end users camped outside new subdivisions and often tussled for the right to snap up real estate which existed only on paper. Developers were known to increase prices as the supplicants stood outdoors. The law of supply and demand, in action. And it happened again as the Toronto condos were released that cold November morning.

As for One Bloor East, most of the line was comprised of real estate agents and brokers gambling on being able to flip the properties long before anyone set foot on a hand-buffed tile in 2011.

Shades of 1989? Desperate buyers camp out in T.O.

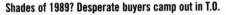

Whether it was an elaborately-staged marketing event, or a bona fide act of buyer desperation, this days long line of people outside a new, luxury Toronto condo development was reminiscent of the final days of the last real estate bubble, almost twenty years before.

— *Toronto Star* photo

For some believers, like Mr. Litvak, it was a slam dunk. "If the building was 160-storeys, it would sell out," he told a reporter sent to chronicle the event.

But the preponderance of brokers, investors, flippers and agents in the queue underscored one key reason why the magnificent One Bloor East, with its infinity-edge pool in the penultimate suite (water will lap up against the plate glass exterior wall of the unit), may never be built. Rampant speculation and the triumph of investors over end users is a hallmark of the final phase of all real estate booms and bubbles. Ironically, there seems to be no collection of people less able to spot housing excess than realtors, and those with a stake in the myth of housing upcycle perpetuity.

In cities like Toronto and Vancouver, the condo explosion was also directly related to the fact that detached homes had become too expensive to buy, except for the rich and the brave. On the West Coast, condo prices averaged $600,000, and high-rise sales by the end of 2007 accounted for a record 60 per cent of all real estate transactions. Sales of condo units over $1 million —in tall buildings and townhomes—had exploded 49 per cent in a single year.

In Toronto, there were almost 58,000 condo units under construction by the end of 2007, about a year's supply, making it the biggest condo zone in North America. For the first time that year, condo units outsold traditional homes, which had a direct impact on the one thing that these high-rise units had going for them—affordability.

A 700-square-foot unit in 2005 took an income of about $55,000 to afford—about the median earnings of Canadian families. But within two years, that income requirement had jumped to $70,000. At the same time, the American credit crunch was affecting Canadian banks enough to raise mortgage rates, with even more cash flow needed.

Consider the signs: An unprecedented new supply of as yet-unbuilt condos coming to market. Prices rising and affordability dropping. Speculators and flippers on the sidewalk. The

"Cheaper than advertising"

While sidewalks full of fevered condo buyers might be a sign of a real estate market gone mad, line-ups of impostors might be worse. Several months after the crowds desperate to get their hands on the midtown Toronto condos had been sated, media reports surfaced that it might all have started as a hoax. The suggestion was made that the camp-outs were staged by real estate developers just to create a media sensation.

Commented a wary *Toronto Star* real estate reporter: "It did seem fishy that we got calls and emails from marketers and real estate agents tipping us off to lineups—sometimes before the lineups had even formed. One reader, who claimed to have flipped nearly 100 condos since 2001, told us that paying a bunch of kids a couple of grand to camp out on the sidewalk is cheaper and more effective than advertising. He added that 'you TV and newspaper people are all suckers.'"

Other observers accused the developers of hot new properties of posting only the prices of a few bargain-priced units in the hope of triggering bidding wars and of justifying opening-day price hikes and competition among speculators. Quotes the *Star*: "There's a big difference between investors and speculators. Investors are good, they create good rental stock, but when you have this many speculators in the game, you may have a bubble brewing."

Canadian economy weakening due in part to job losses, a higher dollar and slower trade. And our largest trading partner—taking 81 per cent of our exports—sinking into the unhappy grip of a real estate-induced recession. Was this the recipe for higher values and a market advance? Or, the stuff of fools?

WILL THE AMERICAN real estate disease infect Canada? Or are we, as so many swear, immune by virtue of our innate northern conservativism and common sense?

Not surprisingly, the industry insists the boom will last for years yet. Real estate boards in cities like Vancouver, Edmonton and Toronto continue to talk up the markets, even as affordability levels deteriorate and price-pumping speculation rises. Major real estate conglomerates such as RE/MAX and Royal LePage are relentlessly cheerful, blithely dismissing changing market conditions in favour of feeding the real estate fantasy.

For example, as 2007 ended in a deepening US housing crisis, mounting unemployment in central Canada and a sharp decline in housing sales in Calgary and Edmonton, LePage issued a media release on the "10 Must Haves for Today's Multi-Million Dollar Homes." (1. Elevator car lifts, indoor carwashes 2. Walk-in refrigerators 3. Spas, gyms and yoga and Pilates Studios 4. Wine cellars and tasting rooms 5. Concierge 6. Media rooms 7. Wrapping and sewing rooms 8. Structured wiring and security 9. Home elevators 10. Heated driveways, walkways and garages.) This was consistent with the company's "Rags to Riches to Real Estate" report issued in the Spring of that year, which suggested "good old-fashioned hard work" was the key "to unlocking good fortune and the front door of a new luxury home."

At a time when the average family income was insufficient to afford the average-priced $400,000 home in Toronto, or the median $600,000 condo in Vancouver, this was the message from LePage president and CEO, Phil Soper: "Luxury living is no longer the exclusive domain of a few. Bouyant economic conditions and confidence in the market going forward have ignited a growing passion for investing in luxury property among an increasing number of Canadian families. Consequently, homes in this market niche have been trading briskly, and this has put pressure on prices. The poll findings reveal that real estate in the Carriage Trade market is both sought after and attainable for hard working people across the country."

The message was clear: work hard, get rich. Or at least, live in a home that will make you appear rich.

About the same time, one of the country's leading housing economists was stating with concrete finality, there was no housing bubble. Just four months prior to investors, not far from his bank tower, mobbing new condo development sites and sleeping on the ground, Carl Gomes wrote, "Canada's red-hot housing market is on a solid foundation because there is very little evidence of speculative activity. While a modest cooling is in the cards this year and next, there are a number of misconceptions about the state of the housing market and where it's going."

Mister Gomes works for TD Canada Trust, one of Canada's major financial institutions, with $422 billion in assets and 10 million customers. Its mortgage division is a market leader in a hotly competitive sector. Mortgage lending is key to bank profitability, as home loans are known as "relationship products," which foster the growth of other products, such as car loans, mutual fund sales, RRSPs and insurance policies. Of course one would expect bank-employed economists to be supportive of the housing market, and Mr. Gomes, like his colleagues, does not disappoint.

In his landmark report, "Bursting Aspects of the Housing Bubble Myth," the affable Bay Street banker claimed the condo market was not overbuilt, even in Toronto, that condos "keep homeownership accessible to many potential buyers," and that an aging population and unique demographics in Canada will not hurt real estate values.

Despite the fact Canada has the largest baby boom population in the world, making up a stunning 32 per cent of the country, with a massive accumulation of wealth in housing, Mr. Gomes does not see any problems down the road as boomers cash out to finance their long years of retirement. "In fact, this large cohort currently spans in age from 60 all the way down to 39. So, while the leading edge of boomers may be pondering retirement, there are just as many younger boomers with growing families that are still thinking about trading up to larger homes and who are not even thinking about retiring until about 2020."

Well, almost. The leading age of the boomers in 2008 was 62, and the youngest was 42. The median age of a Canadian is now 40, and by 2011 it will be 41. The population of Canada is older than that of the United States, and has a lot more money invested in real estate. In fact, as a Statistics Canada report 'details, "Along with Japan, Canada has the lowest ratio of younger individuals in the workforce (20 to 39) to those aged 40 to 59. In no other G8 country is there such a contrast in the population sizes of the younger to the older population in the core working ages. Hence, there is a need to prepare younger generations for the impact of the retirement of the baby boomers."

The Gomez report suggests, certainly when it comes to demographic changes, that the Canadian housing market may well remain strong until 2020. "Aging boomers are likely to reshape the types of housing that will be in demand over the next two decades, but they are unlikely to cause a deep correction in prices." Saying his bank expects home prices to increase annually by 3 per cent over the next decade—putting the average single detached home in Vancouver at $995,000 in ten years (which will require $250,000 down and an income of $194,000 to carry the $745,000 mortgage), the economist concludes, "The return per unit of risk in housing has actually been better than in the topsy-turvy world of stock markets."

True enough. But then, Canadian families have not allowed more than 80 per cent of their net worth to accumulate in the stock market. At the same time, stocks, bonds, mutual funds and other financial investments are liquid. Real estate is not. Shares in the TD Bank can be sold with a phone call, and the funds received within a couple of days. Selling a $600,000 house in the 905 region of southern Ontario in late 2007 could easily take six months, and several rounds of price reductions, with any sale hanging on a thread until the moment of closing, plus a non-deductible realtor commission in excess of $30,000. Real estate's a long-term hold in a short-term world.

Moreover, is it reasonable to expect Canadian family incomes to double or triple in the next decade, and mortgage rates to remain stable, in order for real estate affordability to be maintained at current levels? Is this a reasonable, credible premise for one of the country's leading economists to put forward? Is it equally believable for the CEO of the country's largest real estate marketing company to claim that "good old-fashioned hard work" not wealth or income, is the main pre-requisite for ownership of a luxury home?

In fact, there is a sound argument for concluding that when it comes to real estate information, the kind of news upon which young couples entering the market make buying decisions, that credibility's been in short supply. This is an industry selling a desire, not a need, and doing it extremely well. For example, a RE/MAX report on first-time buyers published in March 2007, spoke of the "undaunted enthusiasm" of young home-hunters, which was "expected to translate into sales at or ahead of last year's record levels.

"Buyers are finding the means necessary to enter the market, even in the western provinces, where double-digit gains have been reported and sales-to-listings ratios hover around the 80 per cent mark," said RE/MAX executive vice president Michael Polzler. "Purchasers simply refuse to be priced out of the market, even though household income has not kept pace with housing appreciation."

In fact it is just that—fear of rising prices, of being shut out of a real estate market that will increase in value forever—that the Canadian housing industry has been using to motivate more and more buyers, despite the personal burdens involved.

"Price increases," said Polzler, "are a reality in the marketplace. One year can set you back—from location to house size—and your dollar just doesn't have the same purchasing power."

And yet within a two-hour drive of Vancouver or Toronto, in the border states, the purchasing power of real estate buyers was increasing daily, as prices tumbled, foreclosures mounted and millions of families learned that the same confident and reassuring words they'd heard two years earlier were now leading them, just as boldly, just as confidently, into debt.

IS CANADA IMMUNE? BMO Nesbitt Burns economist Douglas Porter has argued just that, saying a "decoupling" has taken place between the sinking US and the robust Canadian economies. Says Porter in a 2007 corporate report, "it's a myth that every time the U.S. sneezes, Canada catches a cold. Even if the US economy does succumb to a full-fledged downturn, that does not necessarily mean that Canada will automatically follow suit."

Porter argues that, although Canada's economy is intertwined with that of America, we are better off because of four key elements: tax cuts, high commodity prices, low interest rates and a robust housing market. His conclusion is that while the United States seems destined to stumble, Canadian investors should, well, keep on investing.

However, Porter may be glossing reality. Canadian and US stock markets have been moving in tandem. The currencies of both countries were of roughly equal value in 2007 and into 2008. Central bank interest rates in both countries were in the 4 per cent range, and medium-term mortgages around 7 per cent. The populations of both countries are of roughly equal age. Households are equally indebted.

The savings rate of families in both countries is equally at zero. Inflation has been about the same. And direct sales to the United States still equal about a quarter of our gross domestic product, and consumes more than three-quarters of our exports. In fact, Canada now supplies 70 per cent of America's oil, and has never been so tightly bound to its southern partner, thanks to free trade agreements and the SPP—Security and Prosperity Partnership.

So why is it so many Canadians—including smart, well-educated corporate executives—believe it is possible for us to avoid the worst real asset meltdown since the 1930s, taking place close to our borders?

Perhaps naked self interest is one answer. BMO, like Canada's other major banks, is heavily dependent on its mortgage portfolio. Millions of bank shareholders, like millions more bondholders, have a giant investment in the sustained growth of the real estate market and the endless appetite of homeowners for more debt. Not surprisingly, like the big real estate marketers, their spokespeople have been instrumental in leading public opinion on the future of housing as an investment commodity.

In fact, it's been that transformation—from shelter to financial asset—that's helped justify in the public's mind the asset inflation of real estate itself. New buyers, choking on the cost of a home and staggered by the mortgage debt required to carry it, are egged on by experts reminding them that next year the home will be worth more, and equity will have magically appeared in their bedrooms, closets and kitchen cupboards. In that context, home loans are never intended to be paid off, but are merely means to an end—equity and a bigger house.

The advent of the forty-year amortization ushers in a new era of the lifetime mortgage. Buyers in their 30s readily accept debt that will be with them until years after they have retired, should they stay in the same home or port the loan with them between properties. In fact, if fifty-year "ams" were widely available from the banks, they'd be the mortgage of choice—since the longer the repayment, the lower monthly charges, and the more house (and debt) a buyer can afford.

In fact, extending the repayment on a homebuyers' debt by fifteen years has some profound implications. First, it masks growing problems with affordability. In 2007, there was no doubt that the ability of average people to afford standard houses was eroding fast, thanks to rampant price hikes, creeping mortgage

Same payment, more house, more debt

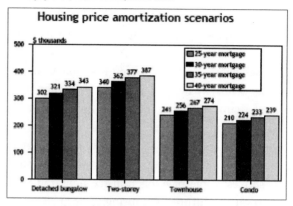

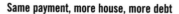

This Royal Bank chart shows that with a 25 per cent down payment, borrowers opting for a forty-year repayment rather than one of twenty-five years can buy more house by affording to carry a bigger mortgage. The total debt to be repaid, however, also balloons.
— RBC Economics

rates, rising utility and insurance bills and higher property taxes. This was born out by the Royal Bank's housing affordability report which said the brew combined "to deliver a severe hit to housing affordability." The bank added, "the portion of before-tax household income going towards home ownership costs suffered one of its largest and most broadly-based quarterly deteriorations in the current housing cycle stretching back to the mid-1990s."

And how could you be surprised? After all, the average home price in Canada soared by 9 per cent in 2007, double the rate of inflation and the average wage gain. In Calgary, prices rushed by 20 per cent, and in Regina by a third. Such large price increases would normally chill the market as more first-time buyers were knocked out.

But this time, that normal braking of asset inflation caused by panic buying and a sea of available credit didn't happen—thanks to lenders like the Royal Bank and its fellow Bay Street titans who simply changed the rules of the game. Mortgages which for a generation were amortized at a maximum of twenty-five years suddenly grew longer in the wake of unanticipated federal budget changes made by Ottawa, allowing longer-term repayments. Now, with amortizations of forty years, monthly payments could drop, glossing over higher prices and enticing buyers to borrow larger and larger amounts. It was a game worth playing, so long as real estate values continued to soar enough to justify increased levels of debt.

"It's my belief we would be 10 to 20 per cent below two hundred thousand housing starts next year, if it wasn't for the impact of these mortgage innovations," RBC assistant chief economist Derek Holt said in September 2007.

Indeed, Holt's report showed clearly that buyers with a 25 per cent down payment and assuming a five-year mortgage rate could actually afford to pay $41,000 more for a bungalow and an extra $47,000 for a two-storey home, when taking a loan with a forty-year repayment, versus one repaid in twenty-five years. This paved the way for further real estate price increases, without removing the fuel of new buyers from the market.

A valid question then might be: How is the Canadian bank practice of giving forty-year mortgages, allowing buyers to shoulder more debt and pay higher house prices, different from the net effect of US subprime mortgages? Both make buying easier and cheaper. Both lower the bar for loan qualifications. Both augment mortgage debt. Both sustain an over-valued market. Both lead to asset inflation. Will they both end badly?

And when the boom does inevitably end in Canada, the legacy will be the same for many buyers here as it is to the south: lots of debt. Forty-year amortizations may be cool in the way they torpedo monthly payments, but they sure make paying off a mortgage a tough gig. For example, a $300,000 mortgage taken out at 7 per cent, repaid over twenty-five years would cost $2,101 a month; payments would drop to $1,842 with a forty-year repayment, however. At the same time, though, the total cost of borrowing would increase by a quarter million dollars.

Gone then, perhaps forever, is that concept of a mortgage burning, when indebtedness if erased and a home is entirely

Borrowed: $300,000		
Interest rate: 7 per cent	25-year amortization	40-year amortization
Monthly payment	2,101	1,842
Interest payable to maturity	$330,372	$584,433
Total to be repaid	$630,372	$884,433

owned. Debt is now a tool for growing numbers of Canadians, not a financial black mark to be removed. After all, with 95 per cent financing and forty-year loans available at every big bank and new subdivision sales trailer, how can any young couple ever be expected to pay off a mortgage? Or even try? Or want to?

Rising home values every year—every month in some markets—make mortgages shrink on their own. The scary reality that mortgage debt is paid back four times over is masked by the fiction that housing is an endlessly good investment and that current market conditions will be eternal. After all, when a smart economist from a big bank says things will stay pretty much like this until 2020, what's to worry about?

So, self-interest works wonders. It keeps buyers buying, despite the cost and the sacrifice. It keeps prices, and mortgage portfolios, rising. It sustains an industry which in Toronto alone employs more than 30,000 real estate agents. It supports the banks, the brokers, the builders and the trades. It is a multi-billion dollar industry whose foundation is the value of an asset which is often determined by inexperienced ingénues like Savio and Hillary who started shopping for a $450,000 house, and bought one for $700,000.

But it's in that self-reinforcing market euphoria that excess, and heartache, are born.

"IF THERE IS A POSSIBLE benefit to the slump," Jon Gertner wrote in "Appreciating Depreciation," an article in the *New York Times*, "it may be that we'll emerge with a different understanding of the value of our homes, regarding them less as investments (perhaps burying the presumption, at least until the next boom, that they're as reliable as stocks and bonds) and more as something all too ordinary. That is, as places to live."

Boom markets, though, inherently confuse the value of a home with its sale price. When sixteen offers materialize for a property in Greektown, a few of which are tens of thousand above the asking price, does the highest bid automatically become the new value? Conversely, in a subdivision in Phoenix, where several homes are abandoned, under foreclosure and on the market at a huge discount to what original owners paid; where investor-owners unable to sell have rented homes to tenants who ignore the front-yard weeds; and where a bank dumps a home for $100,000 less than what owners on either side paid, what determines value? Can equity not be erased as quickly as it's built? And when it does, mortgages remain.

In a subdivision being developed in phases in Raleigh, North Carolina in late 2007, the builder was forced to offer discounts of as much as $40,000 to move new units. But by doing so, every other home was being devalued. "The sales aren't helping homeowners who made recent purchases in the same subdivision," local broker Jill Flink said. "They're just not bona fide reductions,

The magic of leverage in the suburbs

A typical down payment for first-time buyers is now 5 per cent in areas of the GTA where homes like this—in the $350,000 range, sell briskly. In a rising market, those with a little initial equity can score. In a falling market, a little equity can multiply quickly into large losses.

they're lessening the value of the neighbourhood. If you pay twenty-five thousand dollars and the next guy pays twenty-five thousand dollars, what's your house worth? It's less than twenty-five thousand because your house is older."

Outside of Collingwood, Ontario, on the site of a new resort hotel-condo at the base of Blue Mountain, buyers who signed up by the first day of 2008 were offered per-unit savings of up to $95,000 in the Westin Trillium House. In addition, family ski passes worth $3,000 were thrown in, much to the potential consternation of those who had paid full price for both condo and snow. The developer's action has consequences for all.

My community in the 905 is defined by street after street of near-identical homes which have been bought in the last couple of years by a homogenous set of buyers with little down and lots owing. The scene is repeated thousands of times in scores of towns and cities across Canada. The price of each home, at $300,000 or $400,000, depending on options and lot, means each block of each treeless, curving suburban street represents $5 million or $6 million of personal indebtedness.

Buyers were willing to take that risk, because it was perceived as no risk. Indeed, those who bought a year ago, and have since sold, made money. If they put 5 per cent down on a $300,000 unit, and sold it for $350,000 twelve months later, they turned $15,000 into roughly $44,000 after commission—a huge return. But by the same token, if the $300,000 house were to fall in value to $250,000 in a market correction, triggering a forced sale, the net loss would be $65,000 (proceeds of $235,000 after commission, or $50,000 short of the mortgage owed, plus the lost "equity" of the down payment).

Lost on most buyers in a boom, and conveniently ignored by deep-pocketed lenders, is the fact they are buying through leverage. While stock market regulators would never allow investors to borrow 95 per cent or 100 per cent of the price of a security, governments have approved a more extreme form of financing for residential real estate. Yet, stocks can be liquidated in minutes should prices decline and investors panic, while homeowners spend months trying to move properties at ever-reduced prices once new buyers disappear.

With the current Canadian real estate boom in its seventh year, and prices having appreciated for the past fourteen, what assurance is there it will continue, other than the words of experts whose motives are worth questioning? Are we immune? Are Canadian households so much more prudent and cautious, and our lenders more strict and risk-averse?

As already discussed, the Canadian mortgage industry has quietly embraced practices which are every bit as problematic as those which led to the subprime meltdown south of us. Millions of buyers have secured homes with very little equity, high-ratio borrowings and payments made affordable only through amortizations which, as shown above, dramatically increase the principle owed. If real estate prices do not continuously rise, these buyers will have made questionable decisions. If prices decline, even slightly, they lose.

Canadians, actually, are not so different from Americans when it comes to personal finances. In 1996, we both started spending everything we earned. From 2001, according to Statistics Canada, debt grew steadily in both countries and by 2002 had surpassed disposable income. By 2005, for each dollar of disposable income, Canadians owed $1.16 and Americans $1.24. Given that, no surprise that the personal savings rate in both Canada and the U.S. has tanked.

A generation ago, Canadians saved twenty cents of every dollar earned. Today, thanks in part to record mortgage debt and real estate prices, we save nothing. Household debt in Canada increased from $134 billion in 1980 to $916 billion in 2005—a seven-fold increase. During the time, the average market value of a Toronto home moved from $180,000 to $360,000.

Given the clear similarities between family finances in both countries, lending practices and the inextricable intertwining of the national economies, why the disconnect between Canadian and American real estate markets? The answer may be simple. It may just be timing.

THE SUNNY SEPTEMBER day when two fully-loaded passenger planes flew into the twin towers of the World Trade Center in New York, it has often been said, changed America forever. Some consequences have been obvious. Afghanistan. Iraq. Homeland Security. The war on terror. Xenophobia and religious intolerance. The Patriot Act. Fear and volatility.

9/11 also changed the economy, and society, in profound ways. As we know now, events of that morning have led to the possible ruination of the American economic miracle. Military retaliations half a world away have cost hundreds of billions of dollars and helped drive the United States to the point where it is borrowing an additional $1 trillion per year.

The American dollar has crashed against global currencies, translating at times into $100-a-barrel oil, and driving the Canadian currency higher. Government, corporate and household debt has exploded. And a bubble real estate economy has imploded, which by early in 2008 was plunging the world's only remaining superpower into a painful recession which it was wholly unprepared to deal with. Unfortunately, such an event cannot hep but impact on Canadians, from the booming oilfields of Fort McMurray to the idled auto plants of southern Ontario.

Already weakened by the bursting of the technology bubble, stock markets went into shock in the weeks following 9/11, with the Dow losing 14 per cent of its value in just the first few trading sessions. Ultimately, the markets would hit bottom ten days later, before rebounding, only to crash again, with a sickening thud, the following summer.

The greatest fear Alan Greenspan had, almost concurrent with watching the images of the falling towers on CNN, was that this shock would reverberate through the entire US economy, triggering an immediate recession. As head of the U.S. Federal

Reserve, it was his job to mitigate against the unforeseen and the unwanted, and he resolved to take immediate action. Literally within hours, the floodgates of liquidity opened to American banks, and interest rates started to tumble.

Ultimately, the American economy did slide into recession, but only briefly. The Fed reacted by cutting the cost of money—eleven times in 2001 alone—until, by mid-2002, its federal funds rate had crashed to the 1 per cent mark. This was the cheapest money in forty years and along with it, Greenspan took a decidedly hands-off approach to regulation. In response, he unleashed an orgy of borrowing unparalleled in modern history, and stood back as real estate values exploded over the next three years and as lenders gave money to anyone with a pulse. "It was effectively free money," says Bill Davis, of the Florida Association of Real Estate Brokers.

The subprime mortgage market became mainstream, no-money-down and interest-only loans flourished and a huge number of people who would not normally have qualified for home loans rushed into the markets flush with borrowed money. "The fact that the Fed fund rate went down to 1 per cent in 2002 was an important part of the latter stages of the housing boom," JPMorgan chief economist Bruce Kasman said in 2007. "It wasn't the only thing, and it wasn't necessarily a bad thing. In the end, we're going to look back at what happens next to recognize what the trade-offs were."

With the bursting of the housing bubble in 2006 and 2007, Alan Greenspan, America's main banker for eighteen years, came under

"Didn't really get" subprimes

U.S. Federal Reserve chairman Alan Greenspan presided over a historic collapse in interest rates following 9/11. He may be the man most responsible for the housing bubble and its devastating collapse.
— *New York Times*

intense fire for having allowed such a thing to happen, and for creating the conditions under which the subprime collapse would ultimately ripple through global credit markets and threaten to tank the American consumer-led economy. He testified before Congress at the height of the real estate frenzy that the housing market would probably not decline. He eschewed tighter control of an obviously out-of-control mortgage market. In 2004, he made headlines by advising American homebuyers to choose adjustable-rate mortgages over those with fixed rates.

Those loans, called in the industry "exploding ARMs" were common in the subprime business, and considered high-risk, since they were bound to be reset at higher interest rates in future years of homeownership. When Greenspan appeared on 60 Minutes, the television broadcast, in the autumn of 2007, the recently-retired banker admitted he "didn't really get" how subprime loans could ruin the economy. Evidence abounded. In the six months prior to that, more than $1 billion in mortgages defaulted in Florida's Palm Beach County alone. It's now estimated that, of those borrowers who received a subprime mortgage in 2005 or 2006, one quarter will ultimately lose their homes.

As former US Securities and Exchange Commission chief Arthur Levitt would later say, Greenspan's actions created a "deification of debt," with profound consequences.

"It was obscene, and addictive as narcotics," he told a Bay Street audience of economists. "It gave way to a gluttony of debt. New businesses developed to pander to the taste for the good life. This is what happens when trust breaks down—a number of market actors did not perform as we had hoped." Levitt has been particularly harsh in his criticism of debt-rating agencies like Standard & Poor's and Moody's who failed to signal the risk associated with mortgages and loans taken out by millions of borrowers with questionable credit. It was the repackaging of those debts, and the subsequent sale of them to investors and institutions around the world, which triggered the 2007–8 credit crash.

Meanwhile, on Main Street, it took easy money just months to ignite a real estate frenzy as the cost of mortgages plunged and lax qualifications meant loans were plentiful. A rush of new buyers drove prices to record levels in southern California, Las Vegas, Phoenix, New York, Boston, Miami, Chicago and most points in between. In Florida, one investor bought seventy homes. Not far off, a home that sold for $1.5 million in April changed hands for $1.8 million sixty days later, then $2.25 million sixty days after that. Scores of homebuyers took out two mortgages on each property one for 80 per cent of the sale price, and another for 20 per cent.

Of course, it was not just cheap money that stoked the real estate fires in both the United States and Canada.

While affordability levels were increasing, tolerance for risk in the minds of most North Americans was plunging. 9/11 represented the sum of all fears for the continental middle class. Terrorism was imported from the roadside checkpoints of the Gaza to the towers of Manhattan. Innocent white-collar folks were suddenly choosing to jump to their death from tall buildings rather than be incinerated in them. Airplanes turned into weapons, then airlines starved. Stock markets gyrated wildly, with once-secure mutual funds turning into sinkholes for wealth. The economy went wobbly in a single week.

9/11 redefined the nature of risk. It stripped billions of dollars from financial assets like stocks, funds and bonds and sent it on wild quest for safety and return. It also awoke Americans and Canadians to the fragility of life, the proximity of terror and death, the rapidity of change and the shocking uncertainty of the new millennium. The convergence point was real estate, holding out the safety and familiarity of bricks and mortar and its traditional role as a storehouse of value. When the igniter of cheap money was added, an explosion was inevitable.

SHORTLY AFTER HE had wrestled the cost of money down to just 1 per cent, and with residential real estate romping higher in value, Alan Greenspan was asked by a Senate special committee if he feared a housing bubble might be created.

"The notion of a housing bubble," he said, "and the whole price level coming down seems to me as far as a national nationwide phenomenon, is really quite unlikely."

It was the spring of 2003.

Two years later, the culture of denial was still alive and well, with house prices in 2005 retracing the first half of the heady vertical ascent that the tech-heavy NASDAQ took during the ill-fated dot-com bubble. When asked if he saw an imminent dip in real estate prices, federal government economist Frank Nothaft was categorical: "I don't foresee any national decline in home price values. Freddie Mac's analysis of single-family houses over the last half century hasn't shown a single year when the national average housing price has gone down. The last consis-

A bubble, and a bust

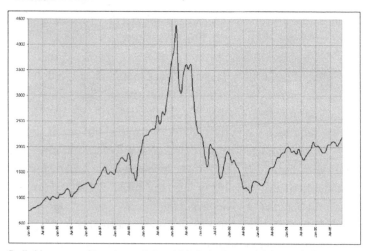

Fuelled by a wave of investor panic to get into technology and dot-com stocks as many profit-less companies raced higher in value, the NASDAQ crested in 2000, only to crash and lose 70 per cent of its value. More evidence that no boom ends well.

— NASDAQ

Another bubble, same bust?

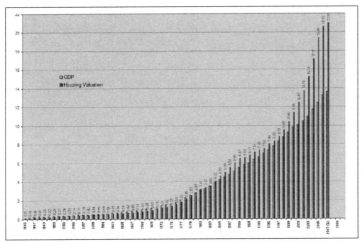

The value of residential real estate in the United States since the end of the Second World War, relative to the economy as a whole. As the housing market became increasingly detached from incomes and national growth, the danger of a collapse increased. It came in late 2005.

— US Commerce Department, Washington

tent drop was during the Great Depression, when the unemployment rate got up to twenty-five per cent, or five times the level we're at now."

Said James Smith, chief economist at the Society of Industrial and Office Realtors: "There's no national bubble. You have to have a huge deflationary scenario to make a national bubble make any sense. The Fed isn't going to lose control of the money supply and take us back into a very significant deflation and cause a collapse in housing prices." Smith also predicted increasing housing demand "for another forty years," due to the baby boomers (the leading edge of which would be just shy of 100 at that point), and "another fifteen years of increased demand" due to immigration.

And, said popular Wall Streeter Jude Wanniski, in a late summer 2005 letter to clients: "There really is nothing to worry about...the boom in the U.S housing market is entirely rational, as is the related global boom in real property. The real reason for the housing boom is that American families are getting wealthier, which means they can afford to buy bigger and better housing, while the monthly cost of financing those upscale homes out of current income has dropped significantly with the lower mortgage rates."

At the same time—the summer of 2005, four years after 9/11 and the Fed's dramatic crashing of the cost of money, there seemed to be more than ample evidence things were anything but normal. As MSNBC.com reported on July 11:

- "In California, the median price for an existing home has surged past $500,000 to the current $523,000, double the $262,000 median of just four years ago. In the hottest markets near the California coast, where two-bedroom cottages often go for more than $600,000, the asking price is often little more than a starting point for a bidding war. Nationally, home prices rose 12.5 per cent over the past year, according to the most reliable federal figures.

- A study by the National Association of Realtors found that more than 35 per cent of all home sales were for investment purposes or as second homes. And even with fixed mortgage rates near forty-year lows, more than one-third of borrowers took out adjustable-rate mortgages last year.

- Ten states and the District of Columbia have seen prices rise more than 70 per cent over the past five years, and prices have more than doubled in twenty-three markets in California, Florida and Massachusetts, according to federal figures. In the same time frame, ordinary consumer prices have risen just 13 per cent, and personal income has risen 23 per cent.

- A cover story in *The Economist* magazine this month calls the global rise in housing prices "the biggest bubble in history" and warns of economic pain to follow. Declining prices in formerly red-hot markets of Britain and Australia offer a cautionary tale for what could happen in the United States, the magazine's editors argue."

Meanwhile, on the streets of America, a suspension of disbelief gripped the land. As one popular New York real estate blogger put it:

In Manhattan, where I live, the median price for sales that closed in May (2005) was 23% higher than in May 2004, according to Halstead Property, a New York real estate broker. The average price, which may better capture the action at the top of the market, climbed 34% from May 2004, to $1.3 million. Mind you, we're talking condo or co-op apartments here—no back yard, no pool, no two-car garage.

Jim Jubak continued, in his June 2005, post titled "Why there is no housing bubble":

In areas where adding supply is harder—the land for building a large number of apartments in Manhattan is scarce, as is land in Silicone Valley, on the Miami waterfront or in the core of San Francisco, to name a few other super-hot real estate markets—new supply is extremely constrained at any prices, and prices for existing housing soars as a consequence… Those who are predicting a housing bubble and its bursting may have much longer to wait than they expect right now.

As it turned out, the bubble started collapsing just a hundred days later.

How could such things be considered anything other than bizarre, troubling, and unsustainable? Why did so many smart people in the middle of this orgy of panic buying not realize that, like the days of $124 Nortel stock, it was bound to end badly? How was this different than the mania of the dot-com era, or the 1970s desperate flirtation with gold bullion, or the fetish for tulip bulbs three centuries before that?

The answer appears startlingly simple—because this was real estate, not stocks or metals or plants—it was deemed to be a

On the path to opportunity, desperation

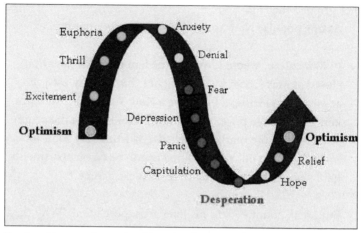

The eternal human roller coaster of investing. The points of maximum opportunity are at the beginning and end of cycle, when buyer despair is turning into optimism. The point of maximum danger is when most investors are celebrating their gains, and euphoria reigns.

permanent trend. In the human mind, real estate means shelter, refuge, security. It has an inherent permanence that other commodities do not. Nobody needs shares in Cisco or a five-kilo bar of bullion, but a place to live is something unique and emotional.

Besides, the experts were all pointing to valid historical data in the summer of 2005, saying that residential real estate prices had never suffered a year-over-year decline in the United States (or Canada), since the Great Depression of the 1930s. It was simply inconceivable that this could happen, without the entire economy sinking into an abyss at the same time. It would take massive unemployment, a rampant deflation and destructive central bank policies to inflict such damage on the world's greatest economy.

But as we know now, this bubble followed about the same pattern as all the others. It was ignited by an understandable combination of economic factors, became a social cult, was facilitated by people to whose self-interest it catered, was augmented by media coverage, reached its point of maximum acceleration shortly prior to peaking, then deflated at a rate several hundred per cent greater than it built.

The point of maximum opportunity for buyers and investors was, as usual, the beginning and the end of the cycle. The point of maximum danger was in the mid to late stages—just when so many new people were piling in, and when experts were saying that, you know, it's different this time.

On December 19, 2007, the latest monthly numbers of US housing foreclosures were released. The increase was shocking even by recent standards—a 68 per cent increase, with 201,950 more families deciding to walk away from their homes in a single thirty-day period before Christmas. Within weeks, the numbers had deteriorated further with word that more than 405,000 American households had lost their real estate in 2007. The news was reported by most Canadian media, but no attempt was made to relate the story to conditions here. And, why? In the public mind, there was no direct connection between housing prices here rising 10 per cent or more in each of the previous three years, or Calgary homes soaring by more than 30 per cent in a single year, or the impact of forty-year mortgages and zero down payments, or investors lining up for nine days on a sidewalk in Toronto to pay $850 for each square foot of a condo to be built three years hence. After all, experts were quite reassuring. "We're not expecting prices to go down next year," Royal LePage CEO Phil Soper had said a few days earlier, "but simply to rise at a rate in the mid-single digits instead of the 20-per-cent year-over-year gains we've seen in places like Calgary. We're still expecting prices to go up at a rate that beats inflation."

Weeks later and thousands of kilometres away, people attending the Arizona Real Estate Trends conference heard something shocking. Said national real estate analyst Gadi Kaufman; because of a wave of 10,000 foreclosures, home prices in Phoenix could fall 35 per cent from their peak, and not recover until 2015. "This slowdown ends when housing prices stabilize, and they will," added Elliot Pollack, a real estate economist. "Unfortunately the worst is

Unloved in Culpeper

In one small town of 15,000 in Virginia, forty-six homes went into foreclosure in just forty-two days at the end of 2007. Mostly upscale subdivision houses, they'd been bought largely by young couples lured into unsustainable debt by cheap rates and innovative mortgages.

— *Culpeper Star Exponent*

still ahead of us. It's going to be ugly, ugly, ugly this year. But in five years, this will all be a bad memory."

In Toronto, Edmund Clarke, CEO of the TD Bank was resisting pressure from the Bank of Canada to sign on to a bail-out deal worth $35 billion. At risk were asset-backed commercial notes owed to small investors, unions, pensions and companies—all in danger because they had been securitized by now-worthless residential mortgages in the United States. Clarke claimed the big banks were not to blame for the mess, so why should they be the guarantors? He would lose. Incoming Bank of Canada Governor Mark Carney knew well the fallout from this credit crisis needed to be spread over millions of bank shareholders, lest it hasten the inevitable in Canada.

In New York, bond-rating agency Moody's said more than $174 billion of collateralized debt obligations tied to bad US mortgages were under review for downgrade. Rival agency Standard & Poor's had a similar story to tell, with $57 billion more being discounted. In a release, Moody's said the action "reflects the continuing deterioration in the US housing market, combined with worsening residential mortgage loan performance and the prolonged stresses of the credit markets." Of course, downgraded bonds would cause massive portfolio write-offs by investors and other bondholders—like the Canadian banks. In return, borrowers in Kitchener, Moncton and Prince George could expect higher mortgage rates and increased credit scrutiny, affecting their ability to buy houses.

In Culpeper, Virginia, came news that forty-six homes were into foreclosure, in the forty-two-day period ending December 12, 2007. That brought to 166 the number of foreclosures in the same town of 15,000 people, compared with thirty-three in all of 2007. Local builder Marcus Bulmer told the *Culpeper Star Exponent* he expected the crisis to get worse before the market stabilizes.

The bulk of the foreclosures came with new homebuyers, and in the new subdivisions of Leville, Belle Parc and The Meadows of Culpeper. "Rather than how much do you make, it was how much do you want," Bulmer said. "It was a panic pace, and nobody ever stopped to reflect on what they were doing. These are people in their 20s or early 30s and it was a very emotional time for them. They heard what they wanted to hear, it was their own fault."

However, as in new subdivisions full of new buyers, in communities all across America, it only takes a few dozen foreclosures to destroy property values for everyone living there. Upscale Culpeper is not unique. Shockingly, it is the norm. And once a home goes on the market, dumped by a bank, it sets a new level by which all comparable listings are measured. If $50,000 is erased from each of its twenty neighbours, then the people on that street are a million dollars less wealthy. If that drops home values below existing mortgage amounts, then there may well be more foreclosures. And while most of these homeowners may have had enough money to put down, and qualified for their home loans, they nonetheless becomes victims of a situation they cannot control. Like Ed Clarke and his bank's shareholders, they likely have no choice but to submit, and lick their wounds.

INVENTORIES OF UNSOLD homes in the United States continued to grow into 2008. Many in the real estate business believed this would be the worst year for foreclosures, declining prices, bankrupt builders, out-of-work drywallers, housing agents and loans officers, and for the American economy, since 16 per cent of all economic activity is real estate-related, and since consumer confidence has been shattered by plunging home values. The reality has hit that, for the first time since the dirty thirties, a house is actually worth less than it was last year. This has struck at the very foundation of the economy, and has shocked a generation of citizens who never thought it possible.

"I think everyone is expecting the other shoe to fall. There's still some blood to be let," said Jim Gaines, a research economist at The Real Estate Center at Texas A&M University. "And historically, a downturn in the housing market has been a leading indicator of a recession." During the housing boom, which ended in early 2006, 1.4 million jobs were created, of which

Millions of empty houses for sale

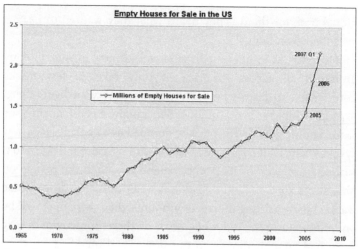

A record number of resale homes stood empty at the end of 2007, a year in which average American house prices declined for the first time since the Great Depression. In some communities, there is a seven-year inventory at 2007 sales levels.
— Office of Federal Housing Enterprise Oversight, Washington

500,000 were lost by the end of 2007. The rest were expected to disappear in 2008. As home values fall, so does the home equity which owners built up over years of mortgage payments and market appreciation. That reduces or eliminates their ability to borrow against that money, as they have been doing in record numbers, to afford new cars, renovations and flat-screen TVs.

Also gone is the "wealth effect" rising real estate values give owners. For every dollar of increased value, says UCLA economist Christopher Thornberg, homeowners spend 5.5 cents that otherwise would not have been spent—or $1,100 in consumer spending on a home that rises by $20,000. And then there is all that paint, and new blinds, and rugs and sofas and backyard swing sets, that new homeowners rush out to secure weeks, or days, after moving in.

Moody's and Bank of America Securities estimate home prices could fall a total of 15 per cent. This also pretty much wipes out the new home construction business, as the supply of unsold homes drifts up to an unmatched level. It's expected this will continue a wave of bankruptcies among builders and mort-

The end of a sure thing

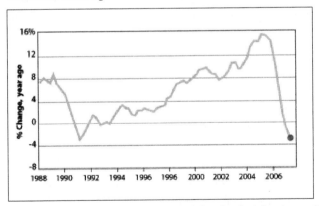

Many homeowners in the U.S., as in Canada, believed real estate prices could never fall. For the first time in more than a generation, they have. Nationally, prices have declined by about 7 per cent, with no recovery expected until perhaps 2010.
— S&P/Case-Shiller National Home Price Index

gage lenders across the United States. In response, Washington tried to stem the tide of foreclosures with its controversial sub-prime deal described in Chapter One, and the Fed again started chopping interest rates in late 2007.

Low rates, though, are also working to keep the American dollar depressed against other currencies, including the Canadian loonie. And while this is a good tonic for the catastrophe of the housing meltdown in that country, by making US goods cheap to foreign buyers, the opposite effect is felt here. Our higher dollar has cost Canadian exporters billions in sales, resulted in hundreds of thousands of lost manufacturing jobs and decimated tourism, forestry and retailing. In 2008, with the American economy moving quickly into recession, expectations were for a further weakening of demand, exports and employment, at the same time as a credit crunch made mortgage money harder to find and more expensive to obtain.

Given this, on what evidence does Royal LePage's Phil Soper stand when he tells our national media, "We're not expecting prices to go down next year, but simply to rise at a rate in the mid-single digits"?

It is this kind of statement that's played such a role in convincing young couples to purchase a $400,000 home in Hawthorne Village, the latest phase of a sprawling new subdivision being built near my home outside Toronto, with just $20,000 down. And why shouldn't they? The federal government itself mandated 5 per cent down payments. Federal rules let them take the money out of their retirement savings plans. The chartered bank set up the forty-year amortization. The builder's agent gave them proof of recent increases in the value of Hawthorne Village homes. Experts like Soper said real estate would only go higher next year. The big newspapers fully reported it. Their parents were encouraging them. And a house had never gone down in value during their lifetimes.

Of course, they'd have no money left each month after making the $2,400 mortgage payments, property tax and utility bill payments, buying stuff a new home doesn't have—like blinds and yard plants—and coping with soaring cost of transportation (there is no public transit in Hawthorne). They would both have to work just to feed the house. There would be no savings. No chance to think about starting a family. In fact, an unexpected pregnancy would constitute a household financial crisis. No leeway if the car died. Or a job were lost. But at least one thing was for sure, this was the path to financial stability. For all its insane sacrifices and servitude and years of stressed-out, unimaginable indebtedness, real estate was a guaranteed investment. A sure thing.

At least they would have that. And each other.

THE MAGNITUDE OF the crisis on the morning of September 11, 2001 was such that central bankers from across the Western world knew they would have to spring into action. Led by the U.S. Federal Reserve, they flooded money markets with tens of billions of dollars in short, cheap loans. It was a bold attempt to prevent a devastating recession caused by fear, panic, plunging investor and corporate confidence, stock market crash and uncertainty on how to deal with a daunting and massive new problem.

It would be six years and three months before a new crisis roiled through the marketplace, threatening to do serious damage to the economies of several countries. This time the point of ignition was not a jet penetrating a skyscraper but rather a million young couples buying a million homes at the wrong time, for the wrong price and on the wrong terms.

The American housing meltdown, itself a child of 9/11, and the mortgage disaster it engendered turned into a global credit crunch without precedent. The repackaging and selling of bad mortgage debt around the world meant banks from Moscow to London to Toronto suddenly had massive exposure on their balance sheets, which by the end of 2007 was getting more serious by the day.

For example, the Bank of Commerce five days before Christmas 2007, revealed a stunning $3 billion loss on securities tied to American residential mortgages, enough to wipe away the mighty Canadian bank's annual earnings. CIBC revealed the news as the troubled US company that insured a good part of its exposure to the American market teetered on the brink of collapse. On anticipation of the news, bank shares dropped by 30 per cent on the Toronto stock market, wiping away several billion dollars in shareholder wealth. Interestingly, CIBC's mortgage division had been one of the most aggressive competitors in the Canadian home loans business since 2001, innovating a "below-prime" mortgage and full financing to self-employed borrowers and others without the ability to prove good credit histories.

More than a year after the American housing dream turned into a complicated nightmare, with rising foreclosures, evaporating jobs, national recession looming and a major financial crisis spreading around the world, central bankers once again united to avert even worse consequences. The national banks of the United States, Canada, England and Switzerland committed to provide more than $100 billion US to world money markets, made available through auctions, and on some of the easiest credit terms in history.

The move had been hammered out in the late fall of 2007 at a meeting of the G20 in Cape Town, South Africa, quietly attended by the Canadian finance minister and the central bank governor. It also followed on the heels of interest rate cuts in the U.S., Canada and Britain, as the financial regulators tried using every tool possible to stave off a crisis which threatened to torpedo economic growth, put hundreds of millions out of work, starve stock markets and put to an end, possibly for years, the kind of easy-money mortgages banks like CIBC had offered.

The success of the coordinated international financial rescue effort will not be known until well into 2008. "Central banks cannot compensate for this lack of confidence simply by injecting additional liquidity," an executive of the Swiss National Bank told the BBC. "On the contrary, the financial market participants themselves must take the fundamental steps needed to restore this confidence." Others see it all as a giant act of desperation. After all, the combination of a credit crunch, wounded banks, falling house prices and mounting job losses all pointed to one conclusion: recession.

"It smacks of panic," economist Barry Ritholtz was quoted in the *New York Times*, "and suggests the Fed is very worried." Said UBS senior economist Adam Carr, "Unfortunately, we don't think it will do much. To the extent that...trying to grease the wheels by providing liquidity prevents broader contagion—yep, that's great. But we need to be conscious of the fact that the root cause of all of this is fundamental, and it's the housing market."

In Britain, Prime Minister Gordon Brown said he was "worried about the information coming out of America," that real estate values were likely to tumble significantly in 2008. British housing prices fell consecutively for the last three months of 2007, due to an unhealthy mix of high interest rates, overvaluations and record debt levels.

"This," Brown told Parliament, "is a wake-up call for the global economy."

AN OCEAN AWAY, an air of unreality settled over many large cities, made up of neighbourhoods, full of houses. In one of them, the historic Boston-Edison area of Detroit, there was much disbelief that, in 2008, mansions could be on the market at prices not seen for at least two decades.

Examples included a beautiful six-bedroom, four-bath, 5,500-square foot 1923 colonial for $249,500, and a seven-bedroom, six-bath, 7,000-square foot period home, for $349,000. Said realtor Joy Santiago, trying to sell the latter, "A comparable house somewhere else would be in the millions. It definitely should be gone by now."

But the house had languished on the market for six months, and the price had been cut by a hundred thousand from the original $450,000.

"It's scary, yes it is," said a neighbour.

Across the river, in Windsor, Ontario, the storm was only gathering.

CHAPTER THREE

"WE'RE NOT EXPECTING PRICES TO GO DOWN."

THE RAIN HAD STARTED to freeze when I arrived at the freshly-gravelled parking lot in a muddy field in Mississauga. Darkness was falling and, miles from the nearest built-up residential area, the only glow to be seen came from an orange sodium lamp attached to the front of the forty-foot aluminium sales trailer. As I stepped from the car, my eyes adjusted to the faltering light. I could see underneath a billboard plastered with the smiling faces of young, new homeowners, a long line of bundled, stooped figures stretching off into the shadows.

The night was turning truly wretched. I walked back along the line, talking to people, almost all of them couples, in their 20s and 30s, asking them how long they'd been there, what they expected when they made it inside, how they felt about doing this. As I gathered this information for the column my newspaper would publish the next morning, a man and a stepladder appeared in the rain. He parted the line, climbed up, and affixed a four-foot-long coreplast sign onto two hooks sitting atop a row of numbers.

People in line watched him, and let out a groan. The price of houses to be built in this field, homes these young couples were queued up to buy, had just increased by $8,000. It was November 1989.

I pushed my way into the trailer against the wishes of the builder's agents. They had electric space heaters and large cups of coffee, and there was definitely a festive air. One end of the unit had three eight-foot folding tables set up, one against each wall. On the first table were colour brochures, offer-to-purchase forms, personal applications and buyer disclosures. On the second were mortgage application forms. On the third sat samples of floor, kitchen and bathroom tiles, and colour pictures of cupboards and exterior finishes. Behind each table was a person, keeping the line moving.

The average time in the trailer: about three minutes.

I commiserated with the buyers, doing what I could to suggest they not be too hasty. Soon I was back in my warm newsroom in downtown Toronto, pounding out a piece on these deluded gamblers, freezing in the dark of a suburban night. If you want to see what the real estate endgame looks like, I wrote, go there.

Within a year, the residential real estate market had collapsed. Average prices had fallen by about 40 per cent from their speculative high in Toronto, and even further in Vancouver. It would take an interminable thirteen years for the value of a home in the area to creep back to where it had been in that field in the rain, in 1989. Many buyers, though, could weather the reversal, since they'd been forced to put down at least 25 per cent of the purchase price and were about to see a merciful decline in the punishing double-digit rates being charged on mortgage loans. Still, those three minutes that night had set many buyers back by years financially. If they had waited just a few months to buy, they would have avoided paying the wrong price, at the wrong time, for the wrong commodity.

Every time I think of that night, I wonder, how did it happen? In the late 1980s, real estate was a popular fad, as it would be twenty years later. There were bidding wars for new listings. Houses changed hands at double the price paid for them just four or five years earlier. Every month, more and more speculators entered the market, serviced by more and more untested new real estate agents. Resales exploded in value. Then unbuilt homes selling from plans in communities ringing the large urban centres became the rage. And, in its last stages, condo units became the drug of choice, since the cost of entry was so much lower and investors could snap up several units with relatively little down.

Many homes closed several times on the same day, the rights to ownership having been bought and sold by multiple buyers in a period of just weeks—each one willing to pay more. To be the greater fool. Sales numbers spiraled higher, as did average prices, until it became evident that average families could no longer afford the average home, especially given the cost of mortgage loans. In its last few months, sales levels in Toronto tapered off, while the median price kept increasing—a sure sign of market fatigue and imminent correction as the last buyers in ponied up the cost of their reticence. Then, collapse.

During this process, it was evident real estate was in a bubble phase. My daily column, read, my newspaper claimed, by up to a million people a day, became a chronicle of excess, greed, speculation, desire and asset inflation. I predicted the end of the party months before it actually happened, for which prescience I was

The bubble on Lake Ontario

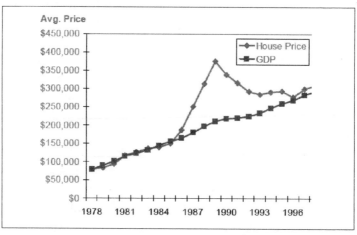

The real estate bubble to hit Canada spiked in the late 1980s, before tumbling into a major housing recession in the 1990s. As happened in the U.S. in 2005, and again in Canada, home values have detached from family incomes, and the economy.
— Toronto Real Estate Board, Statistics Canada

mooned by the industry. The moment of truth on both sides came with a noon-hour speech I gave to the Toronto Real Estate Board at a hotel which unwisely put out heaping baskets of buns during my talk. Agents threw them at me.

Two decades later, does the market pattern repeat?

Not exactly. Mortgage rates today are abnormally low, and quite likely to rise over the coming years—an opposite situation from the eighties. Home loans are also vastly more flexible, and the bar to home ownership has been lowered, by 5 per cent down payments, forty-year amortizations and zero-down mortgages. And competing assets, like mutual funds, stocks and other financial products normally squirreled away inside RRSPS, are now judged by Canadians, post-9/11, as far riskier than bricks and mortar and granite counters.

Today's buying frenzy is also less fuelled by the baby boom generation, which almost single-handedly inflated real estate in the 1980s far above rational values. Today, the boomers are the most real estate-heavy generation in history, with the bulk of their net worth in housing. And while still buying—luxury

A generation of cheap money

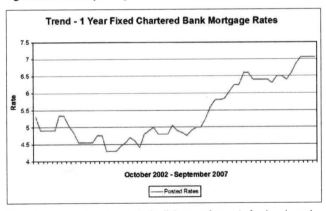

Interest rates have been in the single-digit range for most of a decade, and even the sting of recent increases has been dulled by longer repayments. It's all helped fuel the greatest bull housing market in almost twenty years.
— Bank of Canada

condos, trophy homes and recreational properties—they're on the cusp of becoming net sellers of property, a change of monumental consequence.

There are other dissimilarities. Our millennial society has developed a real estate fetish in the wake of the cocooning effect which terrorism and the proximity of global chaos have created. Osama. Katrina. Iraq. Climate change. Islamic fundamentalism. Drowning polar bears. In such a world, homes grow more central in our ability to cope, and relegate.

This time real estate appears to be more affordable, because debt appears to be less problematic. Long-term amortizations, as mentioned, reduce monthly payments and lower the income requirement to qualify for a loan. Interest rates have been in the single digits since most of today's young homebuying couples were in high school, which makes an entire generation less debt-averse than the one before. It, in turn, treated debt more lightly than the previous one which survived the Great Depression, when real estate values and incomes tanked, rendering mortgage debt virtually unrepayable.

This time, however, the storm clouds also have a different hue. Our southern neighbours are in the throes of a housing collapse. A global credit crunch threatens the stability of the financial system itself. Recession, falling incomes and sharply reduced employment, are distinct possibilities. The at-par Canadian dollar hurts economic growth and provides the country with no competitive advantage, or defense against many American-borne problems. Even our booming oil business faces challenges, as less economic activity foretells a drop in energy demand and as tolerance shrinks for the environmental degradation it causes. Meanwhile, average family income in Canada has hardly budged for years, while the costs of shelter, heat, gasoline, insurance, utilities and property tax have all risen. The ever-brightening future of real estate, then, is linked inextricably with our collective appetite to swallow more and more debt.

And, oh yes, manipulation.

THE NUMBERS ABOVE the elevator car door counted down from sixty-three as we began to descend. Overhead the television monitor carried breaking news of a second airplane impacting with an office tower in New York City. My cameraman and I exchanged surprised glances, and I wondered if I should have added a question to the interview we'd just filmed with one of the country's top bank economists in his lofty perch.

By the time we hit the concourse level, and the car doors opened, the world was changing. Still early in the workday, thousands of people were jammed into the underground space below Bay Street, straining to see the wall-mounted giant television screen Scotiabank employees had switched to CNN. On the screen were shocking images of black smoke trailing from the World Trade Centre towers. Instinctively, Rob dropped his bags of gear, grabbed the heavy shoulder-mounted betacam and started taping. Whatever it was, it was news.

On Bay Street above, it took less than ninety minutes from the moment the news hit that hijackers' planes had torn through the WTC, for the financial towers of Toronto to start to empty. Police cruisers screamed down Bay, mounted the curbs, and parked themselves right in the middle of the pedestrian plazas by the front revolving doors of the great banks. The sidewalks and at least one lane of King Street were now impassable, thick with hundreds of thousands of downtown employees hurrying, often running, south towards the commuter trains of Union Station.

Nothing normal happened on 9/11, even thousands of miles to the north of the point of impact. Thanks to a one-world media, we were all involved. All changed. I took a call on my cellphone as I stood on the sidewalk outside the Toronto Stock Exchange and looked up at the giant Reuters electronic billboard on the side of the building across the street. CNN was tracking the flight of an aircraft, presumed hijacked, presumed a flying bomb. Heading north. Destination unknown.

It was the vice president of the Bank of Commerce. "Wow, do you believe this shit?" he said. "I'm going home. Let's cancel the shoot."

For more than five years, ending in Spring 2005, one of my companies was contracted by CIBC mortgages to shoot commercials. During that time, the bank increased its share of the Canadian residential mortgage market by tens of billions of dollars, and I gained an insider's view of the astonishingly competitive, cavalier and cutthroat industry. I witnessed firsthand how our most powerful and influential lenders create customer demand, spend incessant time trying to grow market share, and use increasing lax or unconventional loan techniques to snag customers with cheap, sweet, convenient home loans.

The television company I founded and ran came up with the concept of one-minute mortgage infomercials to run during newscasts and other heavily-watched shows on the market's dominant stations. We bought huge amounts of airtime, shot the minutes in bank branches, and went on to create a half-hour real estate newsmagazine. My job was to write the scripts, coach the bank executive, appear as an on-air questioner, and to understand intimately how the project worked into the multi-million-dollar marketing campaign of one of Canada's major mortgage players.

During the time of my involvement, which ended with my decision to return to Parliament in the spring of 2005, I was witness to a huge number of mortgage innovations. The real estate bull market, which 9/11 turned into a boom, then a bubble, was in fact sustained by lending innovations some of which the CIBC had pioneered. Chief among them was the "below-prime" mortgage, which offered borrowers an initial deep discount on their home loan, making monthly payments ultra-cheap in the first year of home ownership, then linking the cost to the Bank of Canada floating rate. Since the central bank was following the lead of the U.S. Fed, and taking its prime down to a historic low, it meant buyers were getting into real estate at a time when carrying costs were abnormally reduced. This allowed prices to rise without impacting affordability. It also meant the cost of mortgage debt, and homeownership, would almost inevitably jump in the years ahead.

The bank also was the first major to market residential mortgages aimed at people with bad or non-existent credit. By letting self-employed or credit-challenged customers self-declare their income, without the need for independent proof, it opened a new door to hassle-free home ownership. Concurrently the bank, with its peers, was revolutionizing the home appraisal business, which traditionally had offered the best guarantee that what was being mortgaged was actually worth mortgaging.

As a result, home loans are now routinely approved for houses which nobody has bothered to inspect or whose foundation walls have never been measured. Instead, the green light is given based only on postal codes. In a rising market amid unbelievable competition, success is measured in loan volumes, not consequences.

The first thing visible, outside the glass-walled office of the bank VP I worked with, was a twelve-foot-wide mortgage origination chart affixed to the wall of a cubicle-lined corridor. Every few minutes it was updated by hand, showing the latest, dazzling numbers of new loans generated. I was told his success bred widespread bank envy.

It had also had a palpable effect on the real estate market as a whole, as the below-prime variable rate mortgage was relentlessly promoted to new clients and one with loans to renew. By late 2004, for the first time ever, more than 60 per cent of the bank's borrowers had taken out mortgages with interest rates that floated with the prime, rather than the traditional loan giving a fixed, no-surprises rate for five years. That trend has now reversed again, and my former client has been forced into an unwanted retirement.

Ironically, variable mortgages reached the zenith of popularity when interest rates hit rock bottom and lenders were flush with cash, when locking into a fixed rate would have given buyers years of mortgage payment protection. In 2008, with rates substantially higher, borrowers are eschewing floating rates, opting instead for locked-in costs, and super-long repayment periods, guaranteeing greater bank earnings.

The indebted, apparently do what the commercials tell them.

CISCO SHARES, BRE-X stock, houses. What is it that makes us desperate to acquire assets? Why don't we stop when the herd moves in, when prices skyrocket and logic dictates asset inflation has struck? Why do we think a boom will last forever, when none has before? Why are we so convinced it'll be different this time, with any price worth paying, and any amount of debt justified?

We're most vulnerable when it comes to real estate. Most at risk. You can buy a $500,000 house with basically no money. Not so with a half-million dollars worth of stock. But then, there are rules about leveraging financial assets, and also about pumping them. Not so with real estate.

Governments appoint regulators to manage financial markets, set standards, scrutinize public statements, ensure investors are qualified, criminalize self-dealing, license salespeople and send to jail those who insider trade or mislead stockholders. The latest poster boy is Conrad Black, but the scrutiny goes far down the food chain. Six years ago, as I was travelling the country giving public financial seminars, often sponsored by national mutual fund companies and financial advisors, the Ontario Securities Commission looked into my activities. The osc had briefly suggested I was dispensing financial advice without an appropriate sales license, even when that advice was as banal as a discussion of what class of mutual funds might be ideal for a person's RRSP. osc lawyers and investigators combed through a decade of my books, columns, newsletters and tapes of my television shows, as well as exhaustive personal disclosure documents they required me to complete. I even formally presented my seminar to an osc official. A few months, and $40,000 in legal fees later, I was free to carry on. Nothing found. Nothing wrong. While annoying, expensive and preoccupying, it was nonetheless an example of a consumer-protection agency at peak form.

The regulator was working to protect older investors with, on average, a few thousand dollars of savings to invest. But when Canadians, many of them young and inexperienced, buy a home and take on hundreds of thousands of dollars in debt, they are essentially on their own. Worse, on too many occasions, they are completely misled.

The real estate industry is our new Wild West. Agents selling million-dollar homes may have no more expertise than learned on a six-week community college course. Most agents are paid by commission and often have to rent a desk in their own office. The industry is nominally controlled by provincial authorities and local real estate boards, which are collectives, but is actually largely self-regulated. Dispute resolution is abysmal, and most cheated, jilted, swindled or misled buyers and sellers must resort to the courts for compensation.

Most damaging, however, is the complete lack of control over market-influencing statements, which unquestioning media outlets often broadcast as fact. The results of such unregulated, self-serving and often fabricated statements are playing themselves out now in the US housing market. My belief is we will soon see the same here (at the end of 2007, 36 per cent of all homes on the MLS (Multiple Listing Service) in Reno, Nevada, were vacant). This will come as a shock to those who may have based their buying decision on the widely-disseminated advice of public "experts."

Some may say such buyers have nobody to blame but themselves. But that would be unfair to Phil Soper and Michael Polzler.

ROYAL LEPAGE AND RE/MAX are the two largest real estate marketers in Canada, with offices or agents in almost every crossroads in the nation. Each year each company spends hundreds of millions of dollars on advertising and agent support. Their presence in daily and community newspapers, on television, in magazines and online is impressive. I've worked closely with the media and communications people of both companies, and have marvelled at the authority their messages are afforded. What they have to say is taken as credible editorial comment on the real estate market, rather than potential self-dealing.

Is it marketing, or is it news?

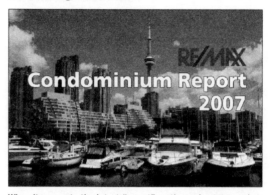

When it comes to the latest "report" on the real estate market, it's both. Canada's major home marketing companies have a great track record in converting marketing materials into Canadian media stories. As a result, homebuyers feel good about buying.

— RE/MAX Ontario and Atlantic Canada

Royal LePage and RE/MAX have come up with the perfect marketing plans. The two companies issue a series of reports each year in leapfrog fashion, which take the form of national surveys on recreational property, the intentions of first-time buyers, city-by-city price changes or luxury homes sales. The stats they contain are internally-generated, verified by no independent company, and of unknown origin and methodology. Based on those numbers, the company spokespeople—typically Royal LePage president and CEO Phil Soper and RE/MAX executive vice president Michael Polzler—make categoric and uncontested statements on current market conditions which are then often repeated, verbatim, by even the most senior and critical of our national media. The influence on the buying public must be significant and measurable, or the corporate giants would not both be slavishly and successfully following the same marketing strategy.

In fact, in late 2007, Royal LePage sought to send the message to Canada that recent declines in housing prices in the West were no indication of any bubble bursting. No recent buyers should fret nor new ones be deterred. That would be bad for business. It found a willing partner in *The Globe and Mail*. "Boom that raised the roof loses steam" was the newspaper's banner headline, with this subordinate heading below, "High house prices are helping to cool superheated markets, which is a good thing, Lori McLeod reports. Still, experts foresee another decent year."

The story, which played prominently in the paper's front news section, began:

The prospect of calmer housing markets in 2008 may sound somewhat dull after the huge house price gains and frantic sales activity that marked much of the past two years. But a return to more balanced conditions—including an expected slowdown in house price gains and unit sales next year—will be a good thing for Canada's residential real estate market, says Phil Soper, president and chief executive officer at Royal LePage Real Estate Services. "We're not expecting prices to go down next year, but simply to rise at a rate in the mid-single digits instead of the 20-per-cent, year-over-year gains we've seen in places like Calgary. We're still expecting prices to go up at a rate that beats inflation."

Mission accomplished. In fact, almost every mission Soper or Polzler embark on seems to end in success, thanks to a media machine in Canada which is real estate-friendly to the point of being unquestioning. And since nothing succeeds like success in the sales business, these two pitchmen go to the same well repeatedly. For example, during 2007, consider these unchallenged statements, which sought to influence or guide the market, and the buyers who create it:

Sales of luxury recreation property "are set to soar" (May 2007).

Luxury recreational property sales are set to soar in coming months as affluent baby boomers drive demand for upscale product from coast-to-coast, according to a report released today by RE/MAX.

"It's been said that money made in stocks and bonds typically works its way into real estate," says Michael Polzler,

executive vice president and regional director, RE/MAX
Ontario-Atlantic Canada. "This year is a prime example, as
economic performance and stock market profits have
propped up activity in most Canadian markets. The boomer
attitude is go big or stay home."

— RE/MAX Recreational Property Report

**Luxury homes now "attainable for hard-working people"
(May 2007).**
Good old-fashioned hard work, not birthright, is the key to
unlocking fortune and the front door of a new luxury home,
according to the 2007 Carriage Trade Luxury Properties
Report, released today by Royal LePage Real Estate Services.

"Luxury living is no longer the exclusive domain of a few.
Buoyant economic conditions and confidence in the market
going forward have ignited a growing passion for investing in
luxury property among an increasing number of Canadian
families. Consequently, homes in this market niche have
been trading briskly, and this has put upward pressure on
prices," said Phil Soper, president and CEO, Royal LePage Real
Estate Services. "The poll findings reveal that real estate in
the Carriage Trade market is both sought after and attainable
for hard-working people across the country."

—Royal LePage Carriage Trade Luxury Properties Report

**"Unabated demand" for luxury homes makes $1 million
tag "simply a starting price" (September 2007).**
Consistent return on investment has prompted an unprecedented upswing in luxury home sales in major Canadian cities
so far this year, according to a report released by RE/MAX
"The consumer appetite for luxury property has been insatiable," says Michael Polzler, Executive Vice President and
Regional Director, RE/MAX Ontario-Atlantic Canada.
"Unabated demand throughout the year has created tight
market conditions in a number of blue chip neighbourhoods.

Limited availability of product has, in turn, placed mounting pressure on housing values. As a result, the million dollar home no longer holds the same cache it once did and in larger markets such as Vancouver, Calgary and Toronto, it's simply a starting price."

— RE/MAX Upper-End Market Trends Report

"Demand for recreational property continues to far exceed supply" (June 2007).
Despite rising cottage and gas prices, the number of Canadians committed to owning their own getaway retreat has increased since last summer, with 12 per cent of Canadians planning to or considering buying a recreational property in the next three years, according to the 2007 Royal LePage Recreational Property Report, released today.

"Our research reveals that the demand for recreational property continues to far exceed supply across Canada, caus-ing cottage prices to rise at a much quicker rate than the overall housing market. A standard waterfront, land-access property increased by 13 per cent over the past year, with properties ranging from under $100,000 to over $1 million," said Phil Soper, president and CEO, Royal LePage Real Estate Services. "Families are managing the affordability challenge with creativity and personal flexibility. Prospective purchasers on a budget can still find a cottage or cabin, but they may have to accept a longer weekend commute, seek alternate ownership options, or subsidize ownership through rental income."

—Royal LePage Recreational Property Report

"Despite Ontario job losses, housing markets will shatter existing markets" (June 2007).
Despite concerns over a high Canadian dollar and its impact on the province's manufacturing sector, housing markets across Ontario continue to perform above and beyond

industry expectations, according to a report released today by RE/MAX Ontario-Atlantic Canada.

"While an overall healthy economy has supported home-buying activity, consumer confidence in the future of housing has taken markets to the next level," says Michael Polzler, Executive Vice President and Regional Director, RE/MAX Ontario-Atlantic Canada. "Given current momentum, we expect demand for housing to continue throughout the traditionally slower summer months and shatter existing records for sales and/or price in many markets by year-end."

— RE/MAX Ontario Market Trends Report

"All regions poised to experience a rise in average house prices" (July 2007).

Canada's resale housing market finished the second quarter on strong and steady footing; surprising many by its astounding momentum. Healthy and robust conditions are expected to prevail to year's end as all regions are poised to experience a rise in average house prices, with double-digit gains forecast for Edmonton, Calgary, Winnipeg and Regina, according to a report released today by Royal LePage Real Estate Services.

"The momentum from the year's extraordinary start spilled into the second quarter, compounding typically busy spring market activity and stimulating solid price appreciations in almost all regions of the country. These conditions will certainly be an impetus characterizing Canada's real estate market through to year's end," said Phil Soper, president and chief executive officer, Royal LePage Real Estate Services. "The most profound story in Canadian real estate today is the extraordinary interest that people across our country continue to have in buying and selling homes. The sheer number of homes trading hands this year has far exceeded consensus expectation. The market continues to show strength as we move into the second half of the year."

— Royal LePage Report

High prices, bidding wars "have yet to deter first-time buyers" (March 2007).
High housing values, tight inventory levels and all-out bidding wars have yet to deter first-time buyers in their quest to realize homeownership in major Canadian centres this year, according to a report released today by RE/MAX.

"Despite a decade of year-over-year price increases, compounded by challenging market conditions this year, entry-level buyers continue to be a driving force in real estate," says Michael Polzler, Executive Vice President and Regional Director, RE/MAX Ontario-Atlantic Canada. "Their undaunted enthusiasm is expected to translate into sales at or ahead of last year's record levels in the Spring."

— RE/MAX Affordability Report

No worries as "steady, yet moderate growth" forecast for "thriving" Canadian market (December 2007).
After experiencing an exceptional year characterized by strong average house price appreciation and record-breaking unit sales, the momentum from 2007 is anticipated to carry over and position Canada's real estate market for steady, yet moderate growth in 2008, according to the Royal LePage 2008 Market Survey Forecast released today.

"Canada's housing market in 2008 should continue to thrive on a balanced diet of strong economic fundamentals, including high levels of employment, resilient consumer confidence, modest levels of inflation and the relatively low cost of borrowing money," said Phil Soper, president and chief executive of Royal LePage Real Estate Services.

The Gospel according to Phil Soper

Royal LePage CEO Phil Soper may not be a housing economist, but his opinion carries big media weight. His prediction for the Canadian real estate is for "balanced conditions."

— Royal LePage Real Estate Services

"Canada is currently enjoying one of the longest housing market expansions in history; however, as we move into 2008 it is anticipated that slowly eroding affordability will cause demand to ease, allowing the market to move toward balanced conditions, with lower levels of price appreciation, and fewer homes trading hands."

—Royal LePage 2008 Market Survey Forecast

It's not surprising that the market snapshot arising out of the RE/MAX and Royal LePage "reports" is one of utopian times for homeowners, buyers and investors. What is unexpected is the frequency with which this promotional copy makes it into the news columns and on-air packages of Canadian media, and the expert status afforded to Mr. Soper and Mr. Polzler. After all, they are spouting some hard-to-belief stuff.

- Hard work, not wealth, is the key to obtaining a luxury home, Soper says, with $1 million simply a starting price, and yet the average home price in Canada is but $300,000.
- Sales of cottages and recreational properties are "soaring," Polzler claims, and yet 93 per cent of Canadian families don't have one, and likely never will.
- First-time buyers undaunted by high prices or bidding wars, Polzler says, even though lifetime debt is being taken on to get them in, at record prices.
- Real estate prices will increase by greater than inflation, Soper says, definitively.

Phil Soper came to the giant property corporation from IBM, where he was part of that company's IT consulting business, working in professional services, business development, finance and planning, and sales and marketing. Before that he was in the energy sector, working for Husky Oil. In 2003, Soper helped reorganize LePage, turning it into a publicly-traded company on the TSX. He is a graduate of the University of Alberta (Bachelor of

Commerce). His background makes him an ideal spokesperson for corporate issues, but when it comes to being a real estate market guru, he has only the obliging Canadian media to thank. In the Canadian media world, housing is a favoured commodity. Most big newspapers have real estate sections, and real estate editors whose job it is to support the industry. Many dailies spin off glossy real estate magazine supplements once or twice a year, packed with listings of properties for sale, decorating tips and features on couples who have turned ramshackle, abandoned country homes into fabulous horsey estates, or whose condo conversions have created a new urban standard. There are real estate-only newspapers published in scores of communities, and the Internet now crawls with industry representatives. Only porn sites are more numerous than house selling sites.

ALMOST WITHOUT EXCEPTION, reporting of real estate and housing-related news and markets is flattering and uncritical. We have developed a collective desire for promotion of our homes, and the systematic augmentation of their value. After all, it would be hard to fathom a daily newspaper publishing a news story quoting the CEO of a TSX-traded corporation predicting revenue gains greater than inflation in the coming year, without at least including the views of an independent analyst. Yet when LePage reports that, without qualification, home prices will go up and not down in the coming twelve months, it becomes a headlined reality. And if it translates into increased market activity, this is not necessarily a bad outcome for the company's publicly-traded stock.

In the *Global and Mail* article quoted above, of the eight "sources"—excluding Soper—all of them directly depend on the health of the real estate market.

The industry as a whole also has much to account for. The Canadian Real Estate Association (CREA) almost annually predicts record sales. RE/MAX predicts a 9 per cent increase in prices. Markets are now more balanced, says CREA economist Gregory Klump. New home construction will pull back a modest 6 per cent, says Canada Mortgage and Housing. Forty-year home loans have helped affordability, says the Royal Bank housing affordability report, and assistant chief economist Derek Holt. And longer-term mortgages are a way to cope with higher rates, says Toronto mortgage broker John Panagakos.

Nowhere in this, or most, Canadian news stories on real estate is there any mention of the devastation of the American residential housing market, the growing global credit crunch, mortgage-related woes faced by domestic banks, the impact of recession, currency fluctuations or job loss on home sales and valued, the hidden costs of new mortgages or the eroding, debt-laden and dismal balance sheet of families. With real estate values and mortgage indebtedness at record levels, with the economy slowing and with clear evidence of what can happen when a boom becomes a bubble and inevitably bursts, the real estate pages and business pages tell clearly different stories.

A stark example came in the first weeks of 2008, in the midst of a global stock market meltdown resulting from the damage being done to the US economy by real estate. Within twenty-four hours of a deep interest rate slash by Washington, a hasty $145 billion consumer bail-out package by President George Bush and an alarming prediction that American homeowners had yet to see a quarter of their equity evaporate, this story moved on the Canadian Press wire, carried by every major daily:

OTTAWA — Canada's resale housing market will remain at or near record levels this year, the Canadian Real Estate Association predicted. The industry group said multiple listing service activity totalled a record 520,747 units in 2007, up 7.6 per cent from 2006 in the steepest increase since 2002, and this year's MLS transactions are forecast to remain solidly above 500,000.

"The results in 2007 show the strength and the affordability of the Canadian residential market," said CREA president Ann Bosley. "The statistics again show just how different the housing markets are in Canada and the United States. Canadian realtors know that Canadian mortgage lenders correctly see that home prices will continue rising."

The association sees three factors that it believes will save Canada's housing markets from the woes engulfing the sector in the United States: consumer confidence, employment and affordable interest rates.

CREA economist Gregory Klump said the market will pull back from the "breakneck pace" of 2007, but this is still forecast to be the second-busiest year on record in almost all provinces.

Average prices are forecast to continue rising in record territory, but the increase is likely to become slower, to 5.5 per cent nationwide. "Slower job growth, not massive layoffs, are forecast for Canada in 2008," Mr. Klump said.

As Klump made that comment, General Motors was announcing a production shift from its plant in southern Ontario to one in Lansing, Michigan, throwing into question the future of the giant Oshawa facility; and an index of trade confidence by Canadian exporters tumbled to the lowest level in almost a decade.

The gulf between what consumers, taxpayers and homebuyers were seeing in the real economy and being told through the media by industry opinion-leaders was widening fast. Where did truth lie?

Real estate, evidently, is a coddled commodity, whose sustained good health is an important element in the vitality of local communities. Local media, of course, also rely on economic activity. Little wonder, then, there's a convergence of interests. A good recent example comes from the hard-hit housing market in Naples, Florida, where the new homebuilding business was all but shut down in 2007 for a lack of buyers.

With home prices sliding and an astonishing seven-year supply of serviced and unsold lots available, area builders launched a "Buy Now!" campaign which equated collapsing values with "affordability" and record inventories with "broad selection." Starting with a small $40,000 grant from the National Association of Home Builders, the push grew to a $500,000 newspaper, magazine, radio, television, Internet and billboard advertising campaign, thanks to donated advertising space and in-kind donations by local public relations firms and media.

Said JoAnn Orr, speaking on behalf of local southwest Florida builders, "We all understand that reporters have to report the news, but bad press has shaken the confidence of people to go out and spend their money."

Ironically, the people were in no position to spend. The real estate collapse in the U.S., and the one pending in Canada, was the inevitable result of housing prices decoupling from the ability of folks to buy them, as Florida—like Vancouver—so richly illustrates. A report released in early 2008 by the Housing Leadership Council of Palm Beach concluded that 86 per cent of local residents could not afford to buy a home in their own community, even after prices had tumbled.

> Despite falling home prices in Palm Beach County since the Council's first 2006 study of workforce housing here, the cost of the median-priced single-family home—$345,000 in November, down from $390,000 in the 2006 study—still remains out of reach for many households, the report says.
>
> Although more homes may be up for sale now that the boom has gone bust, and some sellers are settling for less than they once imagined their properties could fetch, prices remain well above what most local residents can afford. The 86 per cent of households priced out of a buyer's market is better than the 90 per cent of households which could not afford to buy a median-priced home in 2006.
>
> — *Palm Beach Post*

But at the same time, should readers, listeners and viewers in Naples have been told that the "Buy Now!" campaign was being subsidized by the same media they expected to bring them news of the current housing market—information upon which they may have based an investment decision? Would the media's financial backing of a pro-builder campaign compromise its own reporting of market conditions? Is this quiet manipulation of public sentiment any different from Canadian newspapers repeating, word-for-word, the boosterish and unproven statements of real estate marketers in their hard news stories?

Millions of American families have been forced to embrace heartbreak and financial failure after an absence of critical and timely real estate market information which could have prevented them from making major errors. Too many people bought the wrong houses, in the wrong places, at the wrong time and for the wrong price. Like those starry-eyed investors spending eight days on a sidewalk in downtown Toronto outside a condo sales office in 2007, or those huddled against the rain in a Mississauga field twenty years earlier, they acted on a whim and were treated by the media as a social phenomenon, and not as the harbinger they unwittingly were.

SHOULD WE ALL OWN HOUSES?

The mantra of the real estate industry is, of course, yes. But in the U.S., at least, a new penny has dropped. Richard Syron, CEO of Fannie Mae, the US mortgage finance corporation enacted by Congress, told Washington lawmakers in late 2007 that his company had "contributed to the problem by spreading the message that everybody should own a home." In fact, the *Washington Post* reported, Syron admitted that many people who should not have owned real estate, bought it.

"I honestly think it's going to get worse before it gets better," he said. "While the mortgage crisis has brought a rising wave of foreclosure notices into public view, less evident have been pictures of people standing with furniture on the lawn after being forcibly evicted from their homes. As that begins to happen, and it will happen, I am afraid of the impact that this has."

If prices drop by 30 per cent, as some economists predict, "We're all going to want apples and boxes to sell them in," Syron said.

Could the two views of home ownership, one from Canada and the other from the US, be any more starkly opposed? While the investor-homeowner in Canada is told of endlessly robust markets, continually rising prices and insatiable demand for luxury homes, condos, cottages and suburban trophy homes, even when family incomes are stagnant, in the US, depression-era terminology is trotted out to describe emerging real estate conditions. How could these two visions of a common commodity in neighbouring countries with similar societies, interdependent economies, overlapping media channels, equal currencies, common celebrities and interrelated financial systems be so at odds?

Where does truth lie? Is the Canadian real estate market, after years of stellar gains, poised to climb endlessly, in a balanced and predictable fashion, or is a correction inevitable, as in 1989?

The media's answer is simple. The Americans screwed up.

That was the conclusion of a cover story in *Maclean's*, in early 2008. It asked the question whether or not the country's real estate market had reached bubble status. The answer: No. The experts: bank economist Craig Alexander, whose employer, TD Canada Trust, is a major mortgage lender; real estate consultant Frank Clayton, whose Toronto-based practice caters exclusively to new housing developers; Royal Bank economists' housing affordability report; and David Seymour, from the Frontier Centre for Public Policy, a recent immigrant from Australia who claims his under-valued $180,000 home in Saskatoon would cost $1 million in Auckland.

(By the way, for $1.3 million NZD, equal to a million Canadian,

On the market in Auckland, New Zealand

you can buy a new, custom-designed, five-bedroom, three-bath home in Auckland, the capital city of New Zealand, which has a population of about a million and a half, with an average temperature of 24 degrees in February and 14 degrees during the winter month of July. But, of course, it's not Saskatoon.)

Maclean's media spin, is that our commodity-based economy is stable, thus houses are secure investments. "With its bounty of minerals and resources, Canada has seen record low unemployment," *Maclean's* states. "Even in Ontario, where manufacturing has been hard hit by the high loonie, the province has added jobs over the last year. The situation bodes well for continued strength in the housing market, assuming employment remains strong."

The no-bubble argument is further based on our wise avoidance of the three things that the Yankees messed up on, "a perilous mix of overheated financial markets, a culture of debt accumulation, and a heaping dose of pure speculation."

"The problems began a few years ago when Americans with poor credit and no cash for down payments were lured into the housing market by lenders offering subprime mortgages. Lenders had many tactics, but the most popular involved offering adjustable-rate mortgages with absurdly low initial payments. Many buyers jumped in, only to run into trouble once rates were cranked up." Further, the magazine claims that while subprime mortgages made up a third of the American mortgage business, "they never made up more than 5 per cent" here, due to "the buttoned-down style of Canadian financial firms and borrowers."

Of course, this is all largely untrue. And Canadian buyers lulled into thinking our system, our bankers, our culture and our innate northern Presbyterianism will save us from bubble troubles had best think again.

- Canadians are, on a household basis, just as indebted as Americans.
- Collectively, we've walked into roughly 70 per cent more mortgage debt than we had just seven years ago.
- Speculators have been swarming the Canadian market. Toronto realtors, for example, estimate a whopping 40 per

cent of all new condo units in the third quarter of 2007 were going to investors.

- Both Canadian and American homebuyers have been encouraged by agents and lenders to jump into the market with little in the way of down payments. Canada Mortgage and Housing Corporation pioneered the 5 per cent down, while every major Canadian bank and mortgage broker offers 100 per cent financing.

- Cut-rate introductory mortgages have been standard fare in Canada, as well as the U.S., such as with the mainstream CIBC "below-prime" loan which discounts payments for most of the first year, then throws borrowers into the world of floating interest rates.

- Subprime mortgages were not designed for Americans with "poor credit and no cash" but were a product taken up, as mentioned above, by homebuyers of all income brackets looking for cheap money to get into an unaffordable, out-of-control market. That aspect of subprime financing—allowing people to afford homes that traditional mortgage financing would not permit—is consistent with the recent Canadian innovation of forty-year amortizations, which drop carrying costs while ballooning total debt. It's hard to argue Canadian moral or financial superiority.

As for real estate in Canada being secure because of our strong economy, media here makes the argument that house prices can keep on appreciating, thanks to "rising incomes, allowing people who never thought of owning a home to claim a plot of land for their very own." In reality, however, Canadian family income has been stalled at the $60,000 range for years. Were it not for minimal down payments, wildly accommodating bankers, new mortgages which bury the true cost of a home in decade after decade of mortgage payments—and the endless appetite of buyers for more debt—housing prices would have stalled out with those in the States.

IF THERE'S A SIMPLE reason booms end badly, it's because runaway prices seduce unwise people into buying what's already too dear. When the reality of their action hits them, they bail. So, the trip back down is always faster than the one to the top.

Thus, a five-year ascent for housing prices can be largely undone in six or ten months. Those hurt the most are the ones who bought in closest to the market's peak. In a volatile real estate market, just like the stock market, timing matters. Unlike with the stock market, however, real estate investors cannot sell with a phone call or collect their money in two trading days.

Housing is an illiquid commodity. When the price of real estate is rising fast, buyers are often forced to compete for properties, and can pay a huge premium to asking price in a bidding war. Recall the young Toronto couple with a budget of $450,000 who ended up paying $700,000 after sixteen battles?

But when a real estate boom is unwinding, the tables turn quickly, with sellers no longer in control. It may take months, even years, to unload a property in a down market, along with a sickening and steady erosion in the asking price. Homeowners who bought in the market at the wrong moment, who put too

Disconnect: Rising housing prices, but stagnant family incomes

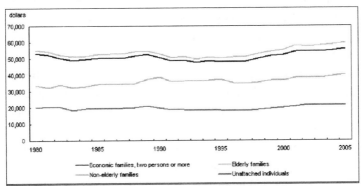

While rising family incomes are often used to justify runaway Canadian real estate values, the fact is most families earn barely more than they did a decade and a half ago. More likely, the same factors that turned the US market into a bubble are at work here—speculation and a new-found tolerance for debt, leading to asset inflation.

— Statistics Canada

little down, who took on too much debt and who realize they will struggle endlessly to service it, are left with few options but to sell at any cost, even when it means ending up with no house and leftover debt. Should the market tank around you in the process, with bargain-priced power-of-sale homes competing with yours, the outcome can be even worse.

Real estate has all the potential of stocks or the riskiest of derivatives to turn into a wealth trap. It is costly to buy, with closing fees averaging 2 per cent of its value, and more costly to sell, with commissions eating up 5 per cent or 6 per cent of the final price. In between, ownership necessitates financing charges, property tax bills totally unrelated to your ability to pay, plus insurance, maintenance and utility charges. None of the costs involved in buying or selling, nor any of the financing or carrying charges, are deductible from taxes (as many are in the United States). Your only chance of turning a home into a positive investment is to sell it for more than you paid—a lot more, since there are many costly payments to recoup. In that instance you might be able to retain a tax-free capital gain, but on your principal residence only.

To repeat, timing is the key to success. And key to that is credible information.

The cold and wet people I met in that Mississauga field in the late 1980s were, unfortunately as events turned out, the greater fools of their day. They bought into a rising market in its final months of ascent, paid too much, and suffered an almost immediate equity drop. Many of them doubtlessly later cancelled the contracts they signed that night, before their unbuilt homes were completed, and took a financial hit in doing so.

Why did they queue up to buy at the end of the fourth year of the housing boom, when prices had more than doubled, mortgage rates had increased, affordability had taken a dive and the costs of homeownership had become the most extreme in Canadian history? Because they believed prices would continue to escalate to the point where real estate would be beyond their grasp. Because they wanted to make money on a house. Because everyone else was doing it. Because it was in the popular culture to grab at housing, and the media at the time was unequivocal in its celebration of real estate. A housing bubble? Of course not. The boom market, industry experts told them, would last years more.

In the late 1980s, housing prices, in Toronto and Vancouver in particular, exploded amid a wave of speculative activity and multiple offers, amid a growing shortage of supply. Real estate became a fad, with a wave of get-rich-quick investment gurus giving seminars in suburban hotel ballrooms and a growing cult of no-money-down investors making down payments on credit cards. The latest monthly real estate board numbers were headline news, and all everybody wanted to talk about was how much their house was worth that week. Many buyers knew they were paying double what others had just a few years earlier, but they believed in what was yet to come.

The difference between a bubble and a boom, is that investors spend money on a perceived future worth rather than the real, useful value of the product. Inevitably, bubbles burst and huge investments lose value.

As has been defined, "A housing bubble is an economic circumstance in which prices begin to escalate so rapidly that the underlying economic forces that drive prices are overwhelmed to the extent that they no longer become the basis for buying and selling decisions (or, more simply put, 'irrational exuberance')."

In short, all the signals were there of a commodity which had over-inflated. When the party abruptly ended with the new decade of the 1990s, there was a massive debt hangover. In a small way, I certainly felt some of the sting. In late 1988 I sold a commercial building to an investor for $650,000, and took back a mortgage of $500,000. Two years later the owner called me, said the value of the property had plunged by half and he could not find enough income in it to carry on with mortgage payments. So, we swapped debt for equity, and I took ownership of two condo units he owned in a downtown harbour-view condo development. The value of these had also collapsed with the deflating of the bubble, and I had to hold them for three years before being able to sell and recoup my mortgaged amount. By the way, during the three years I owned the condos, upscale units occupied by Bay Street professionals, the rents collected did not even cover the monthly taxes and common fees. At one point a local realtor told me almost 70 per cent of the units in that building were owned by people like me—hapless, money-losing investors, unable to find buyers.

Today, some similarities should command the attention of every real estate investor. Growing market share by speculators, multiple offers and rapidly rising real estate values, stagnant family incomes but rising household debt levels, a housing market out of step with a slowing economy, buyers willing to pay too much today for future worth, an industry devoid of caution, self-dealing market commentators and a media glorifying the cult of the home, from headline news to reality TV, among them.

Average home prices in Toronto have risen by a third in the past four years. In Calgary they're up 60 per cent and in Vancouver by 65 per cent. Many urban neighbourhoods have doubled in value in less than forty months. But at the same time, inflation—despite jumps in the cost of energy—has been low and steady, and generally within the 1 per cent to 3 per cent established by the Bank of Canada. Interest and mortgage rates have been moderate and, for several years, at historic lows. Incomes have been flat and employment levels, outside of the boom regions of Alberta, virtually unchanged. Consumer prices in general have declined for assets like cars and electronics. In recent time the Canadian currency, at par with the suffering US, greenback, has further pushed living costs lower by depressing the price of imported goods.

We appear to have a late-eighties style real estate bubble without eighties-style inflation or withering interest rates. Meanwhile the American market is in meltdown mode and Canadian families are becoming less wealthy, less diversified and more

What happens when supply and demand get out of whack

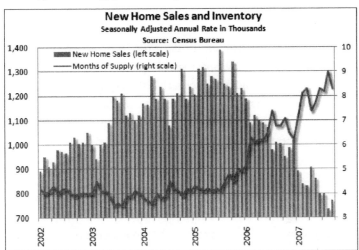

Cheap interest rates, a quick-flip mentality and a housing mania shoved American real estate values to the breaking point. A seller's market turned into a buyer's bonanza, and yet the buyers are staying home. This is a recipe for falling prices.

— US Census Bureau

dependent every day on an asset which, by every apparent measure, is over-valued.

And once again there are people queued up. Being interviewed.

WHEN RISING IN value, it makes owners feel wealthier, more inclined to spend equity they do not physically have. That augments the wider economy, which tends to reinforce real estate values. When prices rise, they also breed desire on the part of renters and investors to buy in. They focus more on future wealth than existing high prices, and often feel euphoric when successfully closing on a property. New owners almost always start spending again, even when it's borrowed capital, to feather their new nests. The wider economy benefits anew.

The whole social experience is recorded, justified and advanced by the media of the day, since real estate-related and lifestyle advertising (home, furniture, appliances, electronics, vehicles) benefits it. Reporters, editors and broadcasters, like the rest of us, usually have sizeable stakes in promoting the one thing they have struggled hardest to acquire, and which represents most of their worldly wealth.

Lost to most, swimming in the experience of home owner-ship, is a longer-term perspective. More than ever, with debt at a historic level, with mortgages which last forty years, and with the three daunting challenges our society now faces, it seems only prudent to ask if having 80 per cent or 90 per cent of your net worth in one thing, at one address, in one city, makes sense. Especially when it is illiquid. Especially when history shows real estate values are wildly cyclical.

Today the multi-billion dollar real estate industry, led by mar-keting companies and institutional lenders like CIBC, TD, RBC, Scotia and BMO, naturally promote homeownership as a positive, low-risk step towards financial security. Young couples are partic-ularly encouraged to take the plunge, and entire programs—like the 5 per cent down, the forty-year amortization and the RRSP Home Buyers' Plan, which allows retirement savings to be plun-dered for a real estate down payment—have sprung up to cater to them specifically.

The industry argues that low interest rates, immigration, end-less oil in Alberta and economic growth will keep real estate values rising. As Phil Soper told *The Globe and Mail*, they may be slightly lower in years going forward, but, "We're not expecting prices to go down next year." If Soper believed otherwise, would he say so?

There are three daunting challenges we face which will impact on real estate and those who own it over the next decade or two, if not much longer. These are explained in Chapter Four.

As we get there, reflect on the conclusion of Robert Shiller, a Yale economist who correctly predicted, in 2000, the coming col-lapse of the technology-laden NASDAQ and the global stock market carnage it would engender. Mr. Shiller began to speak out in 1996 about over-valued markets, the irrational exuberance behind them and the bubble mentality of investors who were buying shares in companies based on their potential future profits, not the cash they could throw off today. He was correct.

In 2005, Robert Shiller saw the same herd mentality moving residential real estate. The housing boom, he predicted, would end badly. Prices would fall by 40 per cent in inflation-adjusted terms over the course of a generation.

Robert Shiller, Yale economist

Further, the bursting of the bubble would, he said, likely precipitate a recession.

Being an academic, and not a marketer or a real estate self-dealer, Shiller set out to understand the relationship of humans and houses over the course of several centuries, and in several countries. He found that every housing boom over hundreds of years has always dissipated—sometimes gradually, sometimes violently—and over the long term the amount of money families dedicated to shelter was about the same. He also discovered, there is no long-term trend for real estate, other than that real estate price gains inevitably end up matching the advances in peoples' incomes.

As he told the *New York Times*, when the real estate industry was still calling him a heretic, "It's very much like studying a disease epidemic. It's a contagion. When it goes in an up direction, it's very impressive. But it can also work in a down direction."

Robert Shiller says residential real estate's decline, when it does hit bottom, will last about a decade. It's safe to say some agents will be telling you then, it's a great time to buy.

CHAPTER FOUR

A FEW BRANCHES IN OHIO

THE MEDIAN PRICE of homes in Palm Springs, California, declined in late 2007 by 8 per cent per month. In Sacramento, a reporter from the local paper, *The Bee*, found Georgia Turner crying in a coffee shop. She and husband Stephen had recently lost a nearby home. "Sacramento just means sadness to me," she said. "Whenever I look at a house, I see an albatross." In Orange County, realtors report putting up open houses every week all year, with no visitors. So, they gave up.

In Colorado, condo sales were down 50 per cent from a year earlier, with the median price falling 10 per cent. A builder auctioned off ten brand new homes, starting at $150,000, some of them in sought-after Vail. They'd all been custom-built for buyers who cancelled their contracts.

The city of Reno allowed developers to abandon their partially-built subdivisions for which there were no longer any buyers. By January 2008, there was a seven-year supply of unsold lots in the area. Even so, it was expected a number of builders would be foreclosed on, with whole subdivisions being taken back by lenders who would dump them at a still-lower price, driving down overall property values. A vicious spiral.

In Fresno, California, scene of a real estate frenzy only two years ago, one home builder was offering $200,000 off the price of its units, from $565,000 to $365,000, for golf course homes in

Desert Hot Springs. However, said building sector analyst Daniel Oppenheim, it was doing more to engender fear than attract business. "Potential buyers focus on the risk that prices will fall further rather than perceived bargains."

In the last three months of 2007, 31,676 residences in California were foreclosed upon. That 10,000-per-month average represented a 421 per cent increase over the same period a year earlier. For the year as a whole, foreclosures topped 84,000, a hike of 600 per cent over 2006 numbers. In San Francisco in the last month of 2007 alone, home sales crashed by 43 per cent, while the average home price plummeted $32,000, or almost 5 per cent in thirty days.

"It's getting worse," real estate analyst Andrew LePage told the *San Francisco Chronicle* in early 2008. "Depreciation continues and makes it harder for more and more people when they fall behind in their payments to either sell or refinance their way out of trouble." Added Christopher Thornberg, also a Bay-area consultant, "More and more of these homes are getting dumped on the market. That puts more downward pressure on the market; that leads to even more people getting foreclosed on, and so on and so forth."

A vicious circle develops when real estate values start to slide. And it does not take foreclosures to ignite the spiral.

And back in Arizona it was common for desperate home-owners to establish web sites to try and market their houses, then promote then any way possible. "In this desperate, desolate, strung-out housing slump," reported the *Arizona Republic* in late November 2007, "it was only a matter of time before someone thought of T-shirts. When it comes to selling houses, these are the days of no shame." Trying to flog her four-bed-room house, Jeni Barton made shirts for her kids that say "Buy my house" on the front, and give the web site address on the back. With a street full of new homes competing with hers, however, it didn't work.

Contrary to the popular Canadian belief that US real estate is in the soup because too many trailer parkers were given mortgages they didn't qualify for, American homeowners across every economic strata are in desperate straits. In many urban areas, the housing slump problems are actually most acute in upper and middle-class neighbourhoods of $450,000-plus homes. Simply put, there are virtually no buyers. As the supply of homes for sale overwhelms the demand for them, prices continue to sink.

More poignantly, where are the buyers? Perhaps the subprime excess was just a convenient excuse to explain a rapidly failed market whose fundamentals fell apart because it was over-pitched, overdone and ready to collapse. As was pointed out in southern Florida, a lesson that holds true for every market, when four out of five locals can't afford a home in their community, those houses are over-valued, and will ultimately tumble in price.

When voracious buyers and greedy speculators bid real estate prices beyond the means of average people, it was inevitable—as it was in Toronto and the Lower Mainland of BC in the late Eighties—that the whole mess would have to correct. After all, by 2007 in the booming desert city of San Diego the median detached home price had hit $615,000, or about a hundred thousand less than was the case to the north in Vancouver. And yet to afford that home, a buyer would need no other debt, $60,000 for a down payment, and an income of almost $140,000, spending 40 per cent of that on mortgage payments. The average family income in California, however—like in Canada—was just over $60,500 a year.

The conclusion: The real estate market will continue to languish. Perchance for years yet, until prices fall to levels at which buyers can be found, who can afford to purchase. In California, in 2008, that is not yet the case, even after price declines averaging 15 to 20 per cent.

"Everyone's talking about the real estate market coming back in 2009," Robert Simpson, CEO of Investors Mortgage Asset Recovery Co. told the *Union Tribune*. "We're not coming back anywhere near 2009. It took about five years for this market to build up, and it'll take five years to come down. Properties are going to slide back to neighbourhood income, so people will be able to afford them. It has always been thus."

And that was exactly the conclusion Yale economist Robert Shiller reached after his study of houses and people over the centuries. "We are in the aftermath of the biggest housing boom in history," he told the *Christian Science Monitor* in 2007. "We are in a period of exceptional uncertainty about the value of our homes. It is that issue now—how far home prices rose—that sets this bust apart from other US housing downturns in the past century. This is more than a typical cycle where the pace of home building plummets. And this goes well beyond a crisis of subprime borrowers."

There is no long-term trend for real estate, no rules, nothing to count on—other than price gains inevitably end up matching the advances in people's incomes. When prices get ahead of the ability of buyers to buy, they collapse. Those who do not see it coming, become the greater fools.

Could it be that simple?

Evidently so. When a pool of buyers large enough to sustain the market, can no longer afford house prices, the market corrects. And that's where residential real estate finds itself in the final years of this decade. The only role mortgage innovations like subprime loans in the U.S. and forty-year amortizations in Canada played was to extend the boom, turn it into a bubble, and heighten the conditions for collapse. By making money drug-cheap, they masked the pain of higher prices, and sucked in new buyers who should have never become owners. This made the inevitable hard landing harder. It will make the recovery longer.

Antioch, California, is to San Francisco what Oakville is to Toronto or White Rock to Vancouver. Not long ago a six-year-old home, the product of a good builder and in a quality neighbourhood, just over 2000 square feet, with four bedrooms, two baths, and a three-car garage, came to market.

Here's how local agent Doug Buenz described the listing, on his blog: "In May, the house across the street from this home sold for $745,000. It was a larger home, with over 2500 square feet. The subject home was listed in May for $649,000, which seemed like a good price. However, after two and a half months on the market with no offers, the owners lowered the price to $599,000. Still no offers, and very slow activity. The owners have a mortgage balance of about $530,000 on the home, so they did not have much equity. After a couple of months at $599,000, the wife lost her job, and they became extremely motivated to sell. They lowered the price to $449,000, which is far below their loan balance. So it is now a short sale situation, where the bank will hopefully agree to take less of a loan payoff as an alternative to taking the house back in foreclosure. The agent has basically given up, and does not even list a price on the home flyer… instead, she put 'call for price.'"

Clearly, all elements of the real estate market to the south of us are in distress. When the boom, bubble and burst of the millennial North American real estate market is relegated to the history books, American subprime mortgages may be no more a factor than our new, longer amortizations. The real cause was asset inflation, and the inability of normally practical and reasonable people to see the trap they were walking into. It appears the trap was equally effective in chewing up the lives of diverse homeowners— from the equity-less first-timers to the millionaires.

California agent Doug Buenz provides these snapshots of his local market, in two broad price categories. As you will note, there is not much difference between them.

In upscale Hinsdale, Illinois, where the average home sale price in the first ten months of 2007 was $1.15 million, a similar tale is told. Prime borrowers, those with the best credit rating, who bought here based on the belief real estate values could only rise, are feeling trapped. The supply of homes on the market by the end of 2007 was more than seventeen months, compared to a third of that a year earlier. Sellers who cannot afford to wait a

Things are not too pleasant in Pleasanton

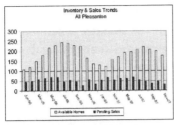 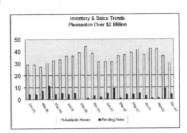

Listings and sales under $1 million. Listings and sales, over $2 million.

While most Canadians believe the US housing collapse was due to subprime mortgages being extended to unworthy, lower-income borrowers, the market collapse is broad and is taking the wealthy with it. These are recent listings and sales in one California community, where people trying to bail out of million-dollar-plus homes are caught in the same equity downdraft as everyone else.

— Doug Buenz, 680 Homes, www.680homes.com

year and a half for a buyer to materialize are S.O.L.—or find themselves cashing out for a hefty discount, much to the disgust, and loss, of their neighbours.

Imagine this happening in Toronto, Calgary or Vancouver. Sales of homes fall by half. Median prices flatline, then decline a little, then are pushed lower by vendors who have no choice but to sell—because they bought elsewhere, because they are moving on to new jobs, because of family breakup, because they need to cash out for retirement, because of a thousand different personal reasons.

The price decline catches headlines, and suddenly hundreds of thousands of other people understand their equity is draining away daily. If they had been even remotely thinking of cashing out and realizing their real estate gains, this might push them to do so before prices fade further. New homebuyers who put virtually nothing down and took on 95 per cent or 100 per cent financing suddenly see their debt exceeding their house value. Many panic and try to sell, worried sick that their losses might become greater. Others give up quickly, and hand the keys back in. As their units go under power-of-sale, those sales help push down the comparables in the entire neighbourhood and affect all real estate. Suddenly no home can sell for more than the lowest common denominator. Suddenly, it's a buyer's market.

The situation only accelerates in the suburbs, where block after block, street after street, neighbourhood after neighbourhood, sit similar homes all purchased recently for similar amounts. They end up being the perfect dominoes in a game of price deceleration, since a preponderance of owners are young, inexperienced and without any financial reserves. When half a dozen struggling owners prove unwilling, or unable, to wait and see if the real estate dump is temporary, or the prelude to something far worse, everyone feels the deflationary chill.

A few For Sale signs appear on the crescents and cul-de-sacs. Some owners try to market their own places, and save commission, while others hire agents and get onto the Multiple Listing Service. The young couples waiting anxiously for showings and offers learn quickly that unloading a house is a far different process than buying one in ten minutes in an opulent builder's sales presentation centre. A month later the do-it-yourselfers have given up and gone MLS, as well. All sellers are soon convinced by their agents that asking prices have to be reduced, and there are many tears as the owners understand they will be fortunate indeed to sell for the same price at which they purchased. Even at that, there will be losses, once the 6 per cent commission is factored in, along with legal and moving costs. Plus, that does not take into consideration one single dollar which was put into landscaping, appliances, window coverings or upgrades. For those who got into this subdivision with 5 per cent down—and that's the majority of owners—this experience will set them back years financially.

But, still no buyers. Showings pick up after the price reduction, then fall off again. More homes are being listed for sale every week now, and average asking prices are tumbling. Finally an offer comes through the door, but it's laughable—just a few thousand dollars down, tens of thousands less than the reduced asking price, and conditional on the buyer getting financing and selling an existing home. The agent strongly suggests they sign it back, work with it. "At least, it's something," she says. But, it's an insult. A slap. Worse, an admission that buying this house was the worst possible decision. It's now a prison. There's no equity left, no pride and no hope. No reason to be here, in the middle of nowhere with sticks for trees. Driving home at night now, seeing the garage door open from half a block away, is painful. Every time they approach, the despair deepens.

Seven weeks later, the owners are exhausted and demoralized. Keeping the house pristine every day for showings which rarely come has been a drag. Watching mortgage payments fly out of the bank account for a loan larger than the value of the house has been terrifying. Seeing more and more properties in this 800-home subdivision come on to the market has only heightened their anxiety.

Months after listing, it's clear that waiting for a buyer to give them a decent offer is the wrong strategy. Such a buyer no longer exists. The gullibles are gone. Every buyer is now a shark, knowing that by waiting, they will inevitably pay less. The only possible way to unload now is to give in, and get out. And so the house sells, for $30,000 less than the conditional offer. On the day of closing, after surrendering the property and the deed, they still owe the bank more than $80,000. On my God, how did this happen?

The answer is complex, as financial answers usually are when they intersect with emotion, desire and the unique mania that real estate brings on.

And thus, consider three tangible, realistic and likely threats to the Canadian real estate market, and the financial destiny of every homeowner. One could be upon us quickly—certainly within a year or two. The others will be longer in coming, but far more protracted and devastating. In any case, there are valid reasons to believe the real estate generation, for a generation, is over.

THE CORRECTION

People buy houses, take on debt and spend when they're confident about the future. They borrow when money's cheap and fret when rates rise. In expansions, real estate does well. In contractions, sales and prices take a dive. In optimistic days, cottages and condos change hands furiously. In dark days, renters are smug and recreational properties grow weeds and worries.

As we inch towards the end of the millennium's first decade, the economic weather here is about to change.

American recession, the credit crunch and a medium-grade global financial crisis are the seemingly inevitable results following the US subprime contagion and the destruction of the American real estate market—possibly the worst property disaster since the Great Depression.

Most Canadians wrongly believe our economy is autonomous and robust. They've been told we have the oil, commodities and resources allowing us to weather the storms which hit other nations. We feel unjustifiably insulated. We think our dollar rises because of our fortunes, rather than the misfortunes of America. Middle-class Americans may be watching a housing meltdown, while we believe houses on thirty-foot lots in midtown Toronto (without parking) are worth $1.1 million, or pre-fab two-bedroom bungalows in Fort McMurray can be valued at $500,000, even when less than one-tenth of 1 per cent of the population can afford them.

Such myths, and the underpinnings of the Canadian real estate market, are now threatened by the housing implosion in the world's largest economy, and the impact of that on the United States and the Western world.

As stated, the subprime mortgage debacle did not cause the American real estate market to collapse. It merely made the collapse worse by widening the impact and inflating the bubble more. House prices fell because more and more homeowners have little equity and too much debt. Down payments have been shrinking in size for a generation and mortgage principals have

Is Alberta a bubble-free zone?

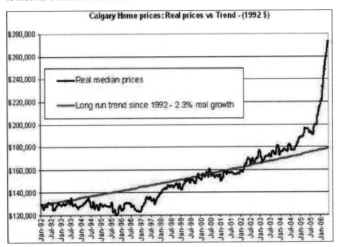

Many Canadians, and a great many Albertans, believe Canada's resource-rich economy provides a buffer against market forces that may cause a real estate correction. This could be a costly belief. The Calgary market's recent activity is depicted above.
— Calgary Real Estate Board

been rising. Half of American homeowners had no home loan financing three decades ago, and today two-thirds of them have little or no equity. Romping home values forcing buyers to take on huge mortgages were obviously part of the problem. But not all of it.

Cheap interest rates and banks rushing to provide home equity loans in a rising real estate market also proved irresistible to existing owners. After all, with values increasing and equity being created every month, why not tap into that in order to buy consumer goods like furniture, electronics, boats and RVs? The cost of the loan was negligible, and the worth of the home was rising enough to basically offset the entire borrowing. Why not, indeed?

The result of both trends has been a crisis of equity. When the bubble burst, home values collapsed and buyers disappeared, the unreality of the situation became clear. There is no free money, after all. Real estate does not automatically manufacture wealth. A house is worth only what someone will pay for it, what you receive on the day of closing. Sadly, it is not a personal bank.

People who bought houses with little down and heavy financing, or who squandered their home equity on toys, have precipitated a situation in which all values of all properties in all locations owned by all sorts of people have taken a dive. Aiding and abetting them were the industry spokespeople, economists, mortgage experts and market analysts—who continue to tell Canadians things are much different here.

Such a scenario hurts all real estate owners, even those with good credit who may have purchased with a traditionally safe down payment of 15 per cent or 20 per cent. As markets decline, they can find themselves owing more than the home is worth. Some hold on, hoping for better days, and content to feed their mortgage. Others worry, and walk.

In Canada, homeowners are personally responsible for their mortgage debts. Banks and other lenders are legally entitled to pursue you for any shortfall between the amount you borrowed to buy a property, and what they might sell it for under power of sale if you move out. You can be sued, in which case personal bankruptcy is an alternative.

In the United States, the housing crisis has tuned a lot of attention on what is called a "short sale." In this instance, beleaguered homeowners sell for market value and if they do not have enough proceeds to pay off the mortgage, they ask the lender to accept the short sale and release them from their obligations. Increasingly that is happening. After all, with millions of properties being foreclosed on, banks really don't want to take title to a piece of real estate they have to manage, maintain and market. Foreclosures cost money, and the bank has no guarantee it can sell the place for any more than the owner.

The odds of short sales coming to Canada will grow considerably as the market here deteriorates. (There is more discussion of this, and strategies you should be aware of, in Chapter Six.)

As goes the American real estate market, so inevitably goes the American economy, which impacts massively on global financial markets and the economies of other countries in our increasingly interdependent world. This was made abundantly clear in the shocking days which ushered in 2008. Massive losses by Wall Street bankers, triggered by the housing and mortgage crisis, infected global stock markets, erasing hundreds of billions of dollars in wealth. In a single trading session, Toronto's TSX lost 600 points while the Hang Seng in Hong Kong shed 1,300 points, with severe losses extending from New York to London to Beijing. The vicious circle that real estate had created was inexorably spreading.

No country is ultimately more affected than Canada, from which the Americans obtain 70 per cent of their energy, and buy 80 per cent of our exports. Recession to the south of us means, at the least, reduced economic growth, fewer new jobs and a slower housing market. Today, with our dollar near par with the greenback for the first time in five decades, Canada has no competitive export advantage which only exacerbates the situation. Our ability to import problems from the south, then, has never been greater.

The correction in the US real estate market therefore becomes a correction here. It's therefore instructive to know what to expect.

- In the U.S., the construction business was hobbled. Sales of new homes in 2007 plunged more than 25 per cent, for the largest annual decline since 1963, the year John Kennedy was assassinated.
- New home sales will likely drop another big per cent in 2008. Federal mortgage buyer Fannie Mac estimates 10 per cent, while analysts at Merrill Lynch peg the tumble at 15 per cent, followed by another 10 per cent plunge in 2009. That will make the peak-to-trough housing price collapse top 30 per cent across America, and near 50 per cent in hard-hit areas like Florida, Arizona and California.

- By the start of 2008, total sales were down an astonishing 53 per cent from their peak in July of 2005, causing the loss of more than 500,000 direct jobs, and off 48 per cent from January 2006.
- The credit crunch sweeping through the financial system resulted in stricter borrowing qualifications and an effective freeze on those with less-than-perfect credit. This knocked buyers out of the market and helped drive house values lower.
- New York economist Dana Saporta told Bloomberg in December 2007: "This gives a dire picture. The weak data raise the risk of the economy slowing faster than Fed officials would like." The US central bank will likely ease the cost of money down throughout 2008, retracing some of the steps which caused the real estate bubble to inflate in the first place.
- It didn't take long for that to happen. Fed boss Ben Bernancke crashed the federal funds rate by an intial three-quarters of a point in January 2008 in a desperate attempt to stem mounting losses on the Dow Jones Industrials, and a tanking of global markets. Then he did it again eight days later slicing off another half-point. Lost on few analysts was the fact that the same tactic after 9/11—moving interest rates toward historic lows—had caused the real estate bubble to inflate in the first place. Fabled investor George Soros warned darkly that American fiscal policy was out of control.
- Falling property values impact on consumer spending. Fully two-thirds of the American economy is attributable to consumers, so the fact they feel less wealthy and more indebted is not good news.
- The odds of a recession are unknown, but the National Bureau of Economic Research puts them at 50 per cent, with the downturn taking hold most noticeably by the summer of 2008. Canadian economists, at TD Waterhouse and Desjardins Group are less gloomy, putting the chances at 40 per cent.

- Signs of a downturn already evident by early 2008, however, included higher unemployment claims, a drop in orders for durable goods, lower consumer confidence and retail sales, reduced corporate earnings, a slide in the share values of financial companies, increased default rates on credit cards, car and student loans and massive write offs on mortgage portfolios by financial giants like Merrill Lynch, UBS and Citigroup.

The hissing of air from the real estate bubble clearly impacts homeowners, the consumer economy and the financial system. "The severity of the subprime debacle may only be a prologue to the main act, a tragedy on the grand scale in the corporate credit markets," was how Ted Seides, an American hedge fund executive, described the situation in *Economics & Portfolio.* The worry is that a new wave of corporate defaults could materialize in 2008 and 2009, as high-yield bonds also sink to junk status in the midst of any American recession. Just as Alan Greenspan's post 9/11 orgy of cheap money and available financing encouraged homeowners to gorge on debt, so it created a wave of corporate borrowing. A great deal of that financed the acquisition of commercial real estate, which is also believed to be at real risk going forward.

While subprime mortgages may not have been the real catalyst for the US housing dump, they certainly have gone on to destabilize global financial markets in a surprising and largely unexpected fashion. In 2006 alone, a stunning $440 billion worth of mortgages was used as security to back the creation of other financial instruments, which were then packaged and sold to institutions and investors around the world, often through hedge funds. This represented 80 per cent of subprime mortgages and almost a quarter of all mortgages originated in the States that year.

Many funds, banks in dozens of countries, and millions of investors ended up with exposure to the bubble American real estate market without even realizing it. What they'd been after in a world of low interest rates was a decent yield on invested cash.

Canadian house prices reach record territory

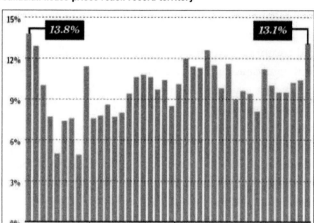

Home values in Canada soared to the highest point in four years in 2007, just as a global credit crunch was reaching the Canadian banks. US house prices began their collapse in the early months of 2006.

— Canadian Real Estate Association

Instead, they ended up with a mess. As the housing bubble burst, due to higher interest rates, overbuilding, runaway speculation, out-of-control valuations and a sea of new debt, financial woes in Las Vegas, Phoenix and Miami washed over the world.

As a result, the Bank of England had to bail out Northern Rock, as mentioned the first UK bank to suffer a run on deposits since 1866. Citigroup was hit for 10 billion, CIBC for 3 billion, UBS for 10 billion, Merrill Lynch for 12 billion—with estimates that the total damage could top a stunning $260 billion..

As analyst Floyd Norris wrote in the *New York Times*, "It was the greatest credit party in history, made possible by a new financial architecture that moved much of the activities out of regulated institutions and into financial instruments that emphasized leverage over safety. The next year may be the one when we learn whether the subprime crisis was a relatively isolated problem in that system, or just the first indication of a systemic crisis."

The subprime shock wave has shown financial markets are more incestuous than ever, more prone to upheaval and instant losses, more apt to shatter confidence than was believed possible a short time ago. As they wobble, a major correction is taking place in America. It's swept away millions of people who believed real estate was special and immune from downturn. It threatens the larger economy. Its influence is spreading. Canadian home-owners can deny it, or more wisely, prepare.

Thus, things in final months of the decade are wonky. The banks have lost tens of billions which, at the end of the day, is our money. The world's biggest economy has been sucker-punched. Real estate is no longer a sure thing anywhere. Most Canadians and Americans have never had more debt than they do right now. Oil is a hundred bucks a barrel as uncertain wars roil on in Afghanistan and Iraq. Recession and slowdown seem inevitable. And yet, Canadian housing prices tick higher.

Is this a time for people, confident of the future, to be borrow-ing more, and buying houses? Hardly. In fact, the near term threats to real estate are so significant, so tangible, anyone attempting to gloss them over defines irresponsibility.

What happened in the United States will happen in Canada. The sequence of events may not be identical, not as swift. But you do not want to be part of them. Especially, given what comes next.

THE AGE WAVE
Like Mick Jagger, Bill Clinton, Conrad Black and Madonna, the baby boomers are with us still. Their influence on real estate has been profound, responsible for the housing boom that character-ized the 1980s, and the housing bust which will crash the market within the next few years, beginning in 2010 and reaching a nasty plateau in 2015.

The boomers are easy to hate, and will soon provide extra rea-sons to do so. There are more than nine million people in this age group, or about 32 per cent of the population, but who control just under half of all personal wealth. Canada had the relatively biggest post-war tidal wave of births in the world, and as this group has moved through its lifetime, the impact on society has been immense. One thing about boomers, they do nothing in half measures. Therefore, the lifecycle of the group has been characterized by boom and bust. Gold. Music. Real estate. Protests. Stocks. Boomers overran the school system in the sixties and universities in the seventies. They imposed a massive infrastructure burden on governments, which started borrowing billions to build schools, pools and roads snaking into acres of new suburbs. They formed families and launched a real estate frenzy which turned into a bubble and burst almost twenty years ago. Then they moved on to mutual funds and stocks, birthing an investing bonanza, complete with Bre-X, Nortel, dot-coms and online discount do-it-yourself brokerages, which all ended abruptly following 9/11.

Since then, the boomer love affairs with bricks and mortar has not abated. Fifty-somethings today have a massive whack of their net worth in houses. As a group, it's estimated they control $230 billion in Canadian real estate, and have a total net worth of about twice that. At the same time, a pension revolution has swept corporate Canada, resulting in 70 per cent of the population now being without any kind of registered pension. The household savings rate among boomers is little better than the national average of zero, and RRSP contributions are dismal. Each year, on average, 93 per cent of all the money Canadians are eligible to put into retirement funds is not contributed. Half the people over the age of 40 have no retirement savings of any kind. The half who do, have enough saved to live for less than two years.

This is a financial disaster, of course, and were it not for those hundreds of billions tied up in residential real estate the boomers would be in serious shape. And perhaps they still are. As I hope this book is making clear, housing is essentially an illiquid investment, easy to buy and sometimes hell to sell. In a balanced market, there are roughly even numbers of buyers and sellers, some price stability and a decent chance both sets of people will achieve their goals. But when demand overwhelms supply—or vice versa—serious problems can occur.

Baby boomer palace

Too many baby boomers own too many big, suburban, four-bedroom homes, while having too few financial assets.

Boomers, then, are essentially house-rich and cash-poor. Aversion of risk since 9/11 has made the situation more concerning, since ownership of stocks, mutual funds and other financial assets has actually declined while real estate dependency has mushroomed. Mindlessly afraid of the volatility of financial markets, and unaware the greatest risk is running out of money, rather than losing it in a bad investment, boomers have been walking into a classic housing wealth trap.

The only way for many people now in their late 50s and early 60s to ensure they don't outlive their money is to start liquidating real estate. There's simply no other option. But the clear danger is that unleashing such an inventory onto the market in a relatively short period of time will see supply swamp demand and prices tumble as a result. Hardly an ideal time to be a seller.

And think about the housing stock most boomers will desperately be trying to move—four-bedroom, suburban houses with pools in the backyard, double-car garages, central vacs, subterranean rec rooms, in neighbourhoods devoid of stores, where cars are an absolute necessity and the local culture is defined by Big Boxes. Who will be the buyers for these properties? More importantly, who will be willing to come along and pay the needy boomers the money they're looking for to cash out?

Stocks plod higher while housing bubbles

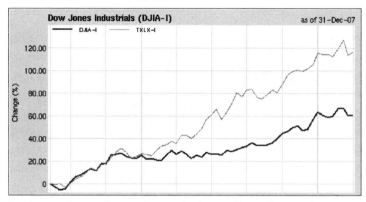

Investors over the past five years have received reasonably steady returns from the New York (gray) and Toronto (dark) markets, while real estate speculators and home-owners have had a wild ride. Going forward, expect more of the same.

— *The Globe and Mail*

Of course, there have been many books written about the boomers and their shaping of modern society. One of them was my book *2015: After the Boom*, published in 1994. In it, I forecast a residential real estate collapse in full flower by 2015, now just a few years away, and a charge higher by stock markets as huge amounts of money flowed out of housing and into financial assets. Since

There's nothing unpredictable about getting older

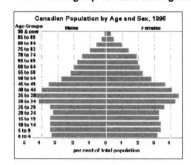
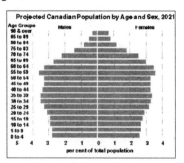

Canada's population of 1996 (left) will bear little resemblance to that of 2021 (right), as our largest population group—the baby boomers—push the average age vastly higher. In a decade and a half there will be more 65-year-old women than 14-year-old girls, and big changes in the kind of real estate that Canadians want to own as a result.

— Statistics Canada

The age wave has already hit Japan

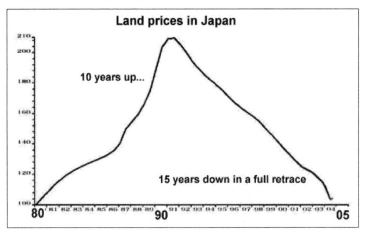

More than 20 per cent of Japan's population is over the age of 65, almost half as many again as are currently seniors in Canada. The age wave in Japan had an impact on that country's real estate-buying binge in the 1980s, and its subsequent collapse.
— globaleconomicanalysis blog

then, we've had several financial shocks—the Asian Flu, Y2K, 9/11 and the subprime crisis—along with real estate and stock markets both going through frothy periods of excess. For dot-com and technology investors, the NASDAQ roller-coaster created riches and rags, followed by the housing bubble now deflating.

Along the way, my predictions have often been challenged, but the outcome should not surprise. There are many uncertainties in life, but aging is not one of them. Our demographics form an age wave whose effects on real estate will be profound.

By 2020, there will be more 65-year-old women than 14-year-old girls. Already boomers approaching retirement age are the fastest-growing demographic in the country, according to Statistics Canada's 2006 census. The number of people between mid-50s and 64 years old jumped a stunning 28 per cent in the past five years, and it's estimated that 90 per cent of them own houses. For the first time ever, there are more than four million people over the age of 65, double the number of fifty years ago. The number of seniors is up 11 per cent and the number of

Inflation, speculation and excess took a toll

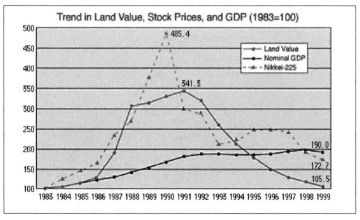

Trend in Land Value, Stock Prices, and GDP (1983=100)

Japanese society was rocked by an inflationary and speculative surge in both its stock and real estate markets simultaneously, and both were seriously out of sync with economic growth. The trip back down to earth was fast.

— globaleconomicanalysis blog

children is down by 2.5 per cent. In just ten years there will be as many retired Canadians as kids.

This has never happened before in Canada. In fact, few countries in the world have as rapidly an aging population—with the notable exception of Japan, where today almost 21 per cent of the people are over the age of 65, compared with about 14 per cent here and just over 12 per cent in the States.

And if you think, as real estate "experts" keep telling us, that an aging population has little to do with housing values, then let me refresh your memory about what happened to the worth of land and buildings in Japan—where one of the greatest real estate bubbles ever took place in the early 1980s, when that country's 65-year-olds were in their real estate acquisition phase. This is not a pretty picture.

Only in the last year or two have real estate values in Japan started to improve a little, after more than a decade and a half of decline. What happened there was a classic case of asset inflation, as has just occurred in the United States, and which has been ongoing in Canada.

You can see in the chart that the housing bubble was extreme, tracing the collapse in the national stock market, and seriously out of step with general economic growth. This is one of the dangers of asset inflation—a wild swing to over-valuation, following by a wild swing that always over-corrects. This lurch destroyed the wealth of millions of middle-class Japanese investors who, more than a decade ago, thought they were doing the correct, reasonable and prudent thing by putting their money into residential real estate.

A telling story, as reported in the *New York Times*: "So Mr. Nakashima, a Tokyo city government employee who was then 36, took out a loan for almost the entire $400,000 price of a cramped four-bedroom apartment. With property values rising at double-digit rates, he would easily earn back the loan and then some when he decided to sell.

Or so he thought. Not long after he bought the apartment, Japan's property market collapsed. Today, the apartment is worth half what he paid. He said he would like to move closer to the city but cannot: the sale price would not cover the $300,000 he still owes the bank."

Japan is not Canada. But that country's aging population—about ten years ahead of ours—gives us a glimpse of what to expect. And these are valid questions: When a third of the Canadian population is retired, sitting on $230 billion in real estate, with seven out of ten devoid of a pension, will they be selling off the house? Downsizing? Moving closer to hospitals and transit routes? Trying to adjust to the climate change crisis and the energy crunch? Saving on escalating property taxes? Cashing out their tax-free real estate capital gains?

Remarkably, the Canadian real estate industry has consistently attempted to portray our demographic footprint as nothing but bullish for housing. A report issued by RE/MAX and Clayton Research in 2001 made this bold statement: "With demand for residential housing poised for take off, robust activity, rising prices and a stable investment climate will characterize key housing markets across the country from 2001 to 2011." This is noteworthy, seeing the boomers in 2011 will be between 45 and 66 years of age. Most of them are already homeowners, which means for the market to be "robust" with "rising prices," they'll have to be buying, as actively as selling. But who will they be selling to? With data clearly showing most working Canadians today are living hand-to-mouth, with no savings and debt exceeding annual disposable income, where will the billions come from to allow boomers the seamless ability to trade down the suburban McMansions to urban townhouses, condos or retirement bungalows? This question is underscored by the great global credit and mortgage mess swirling in the wake of the American subprime meltdown. Are bankers about to extend oodles more credit to equity-shy families wanting bigger, more expensive houses? Or will there even be such a demand, given the environmentally challenging days ahead?

But the industry is undeterred. In the Spring of 2007, RE/MAX was at it again in the recreational property market report referenced in Chapter Three. It asserted sales of cottages, hobby farms and cabins on rivers were "about to soar" as "affluent" boomers charged into the Canadian landscape.

"Baby boomers are investing in the future—from both a lifestyle perspective and an economic standpoint," says Elton Ash, Regional Director, RE/MAX of Western Canada. "Tremendous equity gains have been realized in recent years as demand for recreational properties across the country swells. Given the aging of the population, this trend is expected to continue for at least the next five to ten years as baby boomers move through the cycle."

This now suggests boomer demand will continue to move real estate, at least recreational properties, from 2007 to at least 2012, and likely 2017. At that time the lead edge of the boomers will be seventy. Not to be outdone, economist Craig Alexander, of TD Canada Trust—the big mortgage lender—weighed in with a mid-2006 report forecasting a 4 per cent annual increase in home prices over the next twenty-five years. That would put the average house in Toronto at just over $1 million, the average Calgary home at $1.4 million and the average detached Vancouver residence at $2.2 million. In order to afford a Toronto property, a buyer would need $250,000 in cash and an annual income of more than $190,000. To live in Vancouver, an income of almost $400,000.

"Fears the baby boomers will depress housing prices as they sell their properties and move into retirement homes are likely overblown," Alexander wrote. "Individuals are living longer, healthier lives. The aging population could actually lead to a modest rise in the national home ownership rate. The implication is that slower household formation may temper home price growth, but the implication should be gradual and only moderate."

But lost in the bank commentary is the question of what nine million aging, retiring Canadians will be living on in a world leading us to average million-dollar houses. With the Canada Pension Plan providing enough money for just groceries and gas for a couple (the maximum benefit is less than $900 a month), and with the vast majority of people having no employment-related income, why on earth would they continue to sit on billions in home equity? Some may do so, of course, believing in the vision the bankers spin, but many—millions—will not be so gullible. They simply do not have a choice. They will be selling, praying for an offer, getting out at any price.

Then, of course, there is the wider economy to consider. A rapidly aging population with an unprecedented rise in the number of retired people is not a recipe for productivity gains. Health care costs alone could be a daunting future roadblock.

It's been calculated that if taxes remain at current levels, there could be an unfunded liability for health care expenditures of $531 billion by the year 2040. That's huge, equaling about half the economy, and it begs the question: Where will it come from? Will taxes have to rise on working families to pay for the new hips, knees and corneas boomers need so they can maintain their lifestyles? Will the system of public health care break down? Will we move to a user-pay or two-tier system in which real estate-strapped and cash-shy retirees have to pay for their own new body parts?

And why are we not speaking of such things now? Coming up with a plan? After all, boomers currently control Parliament.

In Britain, where there is also a large baby boom generation, and people are turning 60 at the rate of almost three thousand a day, it's commonly called the "savings hole." There, as in Canada, the bulk of net worth is invested in residential real estate. A report by The Prudential estimates almost thirteen million British boomers expect to live off the proceeds of their property sale for the rest of their lives. With so many poised to sell, there's the widespread expectation this will knock down real estate values for years to come, especially for larger houses, where supply will outstrip demand. Ironically, with so many boomers looking to unlock equity and at the same time downsize into homes that are manageable, affordable and have a smaller environmental impact, there could be competition with first-time buyers, pushing prices up for starter homes.

Should the same happen here, and there's every reason to expect so, it could be a nightmare scenario for boomers who fail to see what's coming. Those who hang on too long to that four-bedroom suburban palace with the wearing and expensive outside maintenance, the onerous big hydro and natural gas bills, the property taxes which keep escalating, could sell into a crashing market for such real estate, only to get into a bidding war for cheap urban condos and bungalows. In the end, the equity they counted on, lost.

Meanwhile, can millions of motivated sellers flooding the market with millions of houses be positive for prices? How much of the hundreds of billions the boomers have carefully placed inside their homes ever be freed up for living? How much will be lost to a market reversal of their own making? How long will it take after the boomers exit real estate for things to recover? Months? Decades? As long as in Japan?

The answers may not yet be clear. When they are, it will be too late.

MANAGED COLLAPSE

The third great threat to homeowners, real estate investors and the great global property market is, by far, the most devastating. We should all pray it does not come to pass, and work to ensure so. However, the clock may already be against us. As alarmist as this may seem, don't ignore it.

Concurrent with the rise of residential real estate as an asset class, and not just a place to live, has been the most significant, widespread environmental degradation in earth's history. Not only have we created deserts where forests once stood, polluted great bodies of fresh water, turned areas like northern Alberta into toxic slag dumps, destroyed the air above urban China, manufactured tons of radioactive waste that will pollute for thousands of years, buried billions of tons of garbage in shallow, leaky graves, eradicated thousands of species of animals and rapidly over-populated the only planet we have, but we've also—by our actions—changed the climate. The consequences, if somehow the course of events is not altered, will be devastating. First, there will be environmental and economic effects. Soon afterwards, long-lasting societal impact. Odds are, the last thing people in twenty years will be worrying about will be the value of their houses.

Climate change is bathed in controversy. Some people, and most scientists, call it a disaster of unmitigated scope. Others deny humans have anything to do with changes in temperature, weather or climate, and thus argue our economy will be ruined if we try to fight a ghost.

Regardless of your beliefs, our changing climate will affect real estate at a minimum, and likely the very way you and your children live. Potentially, it will wipe away the value of trillions of dollars in property far sooner than the time in which today's new homebuyers will have paid off half their mortgage.

Some events to consider:

- Fifty thousand people died in recent heat waves which swept through Europe. Thousands of others died from heat exhaustion in the great American cities of Chicago and New York. Inner-city property values have since decreased.
- Estimates of the damage that Hurricane Katrina cost when it slammed into the U.S. Gulf coast range as high as $135 billion. Louisiana lost 15 per cent of its total income after that event. Real estate values have been decimated in areas now deemed to be at high risk of similar storms, such as Louisiana and Alabama. As reported in the Alabama *Press Register*, "one investor bought a house on Bon Secour River for $992,000 in May 2005 and tried to flip it for $1.2 million. Then Hurricane Katrina hit. The house wasn't damaged...but now it's on the market for $650,000."
- Climate change which has already taken place (the world is about 1 degree Celsius warmer) has made heat waves at least twice as likely. It's expected further warming will result in a population shift, and changing real estate values.
- In 2005 natural catastrophes caused $225 billion in damage worldwide, severely stressing insurance companies and raising property coverage rates on a global basis.
- Increased heat waves have catapulted summer demand for electric power

The face of climate change in British Columbia

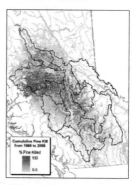

Cumulative Pine Kill
from 1999 to 2005
% Pine Killed
100
0.5

Milder winters, thanks to climate change, have allowed pine beetles to survive the season, and spread with alarming rapidity. They now threaten more than $40 billion in lumber, and are costing towns their livelihood. Climate change, in all its forms, promises a major impact on real estate.
— BC Ministry of Forests

higher, raising energy costs for all homeowners and leading to brownouts even in hydro-rich Ontario.

- Higher temperatures are hastening the spread of mosquitoes which transmit malaria in some countries, and diseases such as West Nile Virus in eastern North America. Severe negative consequence for property values are expected, as buyers avoid disease-prone areas.
- Climate change has caused milder winters in Western Canada, so the spread of the mountain pine beetle has continued unabated (they normally freeze to death in winter). The costs have been huge to the forestry industry, putting at risk $43 billion worth of lumber projects, or six times the value of annual Canadian softwood lumber exports. By 2013, 80 per cent of BC's pine forest is expected to be dead. The impact on local communities—and local real estate values— will be obvious.

Beyond these obvious physical events and the impact on the value people place on land and buildings, there are many other worrisome aspects to climate change. Warmer temperatures are killing off species and changing migration patterns of birds and animals, so that even many field birds have disappeared from the meadows of Alberta and southern Ontario. Canada's north is showing some of the most tangible signs, with melting permafrost ruining the foundations of buildings, a drastically shrinking ice cap and the complete eradication of polar bears from many areas in which they have lived for thousands of years. The incidence of damaging winter storms along Canada's east coast, devastating wind storms in BC—responsible for historic damage in Vancouver's Stanley Park in 2006—and flooding in the Lower Mainland, has increased markedly.

Scientists believe these are all first signs of the changes man has created. Within thirty years or less, the planet will have warmed by about two degrees. The consequences can be expected to be about fourfold of those we see today. They will include the melting of virtually all glaciers, declining crop yields, rising sea levels, threatening parts of London, New York, Cairo and Tokyo, a sudden shift in weather patterns, the migration of millions of people, the extinction of between 15 per cent and 40 per cent of all species of animals, major agricultural losses and an impact on global financial markets through human disruption and the untold impact on insurance costs.

These are some conclusions of the most authoritative and impartial analysis of the impact of climate change, the seven hundred-page opus written by economist Nicholas Stern for the British government, released in late 2006. In it, Stern was brutal in his assessment of the economic costs of the world doing little, or nothing, to change its habits, and called climate change, "the greatest market failure the world has ever seen." Stern's solution is to invest 1 per cent of the world's gross domestic product to avoid further effects. Failure to do so, he concluded, would eventually cost about 20 per cent of global GDP, and likely throw the planet into a 1930s-style depression.

Stern argues for environmental taxes, strict caps on the industrial emission of greenhouse gases—ultimately dropping them 80 per cent below current levels—and for the creation of carbon markets which will allow costs of halting climate change to be shared around the world. To date, 70 per cent of the problem has been caused by activities in the rich nations of North America and Europe, and going forward it will all be made far worse by the developing nations of Asia and Africa. Hence, Stern says, this requires a planetary solution, and the agreement by wealthy industrial countries to not only stop emitting, but to shoulder part of the responsibility for all peoples, and their past actions.

Admittedly, there will be economic consequences of acting, but also of not acting. Capping emissions could mean lost jobs in the auto sector in Ontario and Alberta's oil sands, for example, higher gasoline and natural gas costs for every homeowner in Canada and perhaps higher personal taxes if the government enters into a global carbon market. Fighting climate change could well mean a financial sacrifice imposed on every family, a drop in our overall living standards, sharply higher utility bills for home-owners and consequent pressure on real estate values. It's difficult indeed to see an immediate financial upside to the task at hand.

But the costs of inaction are equally unpalatable, if not fright-eningly worse. In 2008, the debate in Canada rages on a national approach to climate change, as it does in the United States. Administrations in both countries have been unwilling to make the difficult and politically expensive decisions to adopt measures which will immediately impact voters, for the sake of their chil-dren and grandchildren. As the Stern Report said, "If nothing is done to slow the process of warming, the grandchildren of today's young adults will inherit a world crippled by food and water shortages, extreme and varied weather, extinctions and other ecosystem damages, and a growing danger of an even more severe catastrophe."

Stern also made it clear in his report to the British government that there is already nothing that can be done to prevent, by 2020, the number of heat emergency days in London each summer doubling, more extreme storms and floods, and a 16 per cent increase in required electric power, costing about $10 billion a year. Logic dictates the same can be forecast for Canadian cities sitting on similar latitudes.

But climate change—what is already inevitable, and the ques-tionable ability of the world's leaders to stop what is coming—may form but part of the threat of managed collapse which all real estate investors should be aware of. A further view of our future may have been glimpsed in 2003.

At 4:30 PM on the afternoon of August 14, I was in my office on Bay Street in downtown Toronto, adjacent to the studios in which network television shows were produced by my produc-tion company. The power failed, a very uncharacteristic event for that location. After a few minutes a camera crew which had been out on a location shoot came back to report no electricity any-where in the downtown core.

I called my wife at our home in Caledon, a rural area about eighty kilometres away. She said the power had quit about 4:30 pm, and the generator had kicked in. That unit had been installed with some care—propane-powered, anchored in concrete, in its own building and powerful enough to take over the entire load of our residence. I was suddenly pleased at having gone to the expense, but alarmed a power outage affecting Toronto Hydro could also have hit Ontario Hydro, our rural supplier, at precisely the same moment. Something was clearly, seriously wrong. Of course, without power there was no television, no radio, no Internet access. No information flowing into my highly-wired, high-tech office.

I left, walking down the stairwell of my building and onto the sidewalk, which was uncommonly busy. Bay Street, heading south to the expressways out of the city, was also bumper-to-bumper. But then again, it was five o'clock. Rush hour.

Reaching the parking garage I was unable to get to my car in the usual fashion, by elevator, so I walked down an exit ramp several levels until I reached it. Then, in total darkness, I threaded my way upward with a fleet of other vehicles. The streets above were now completely gridlocked, and the news blaring out of the car radio was of a massive power outage which had affected the entire eastern half of North America. It was a stunning and unprecedented event, and instilled fear. Just two years after 9/11, the obvious first thought of everyone was another terrorist attack, this time against the cables or power plants that provided energy to our modern lives and upon which we were totally dependent.

Just how dependent became apparent to me and millions of others over the next dozens of hours. Without signal lights to restrict and regulate the flow of traffic, city streets were virtually impassable. A few police were evident in some intersections, good Samaritan citizens in others, wearing fluorescent vests the cops had tossed them while driving past. Without power to many cell phone relay towers, and others overloaded, mobile phones were useless. Without functioning computers, gas stations couldn't process credit card transactions, or activate self-serve pumps. Even the most elderly of filling stations were unable to use their pumps, which employ electric motors. Without power, stores everywhere closed. Debit cards and credit cards did not work. People without cash in their pockets couldn't buy anything, nor could they obtain paper money from bank machines, which were also disabled.

Grocery stores closed immediately, unable to sell bar-coded merchandise to customers. Smokers could not get smokes, drinkers were without drinks, pets without pet food. In Toronto that day it was 88° F (31° C) and a whole lot hotter inside vehicles, and in office buildings with sealed windows and climate control systems.

As I inched my way towards the elevated highway out of the city centre, my partner was back in the parking garage I'd left, in the sad realization he'd forgotten to gas up his Ford Explorer on the way in to work that morning. He ended up finding a piece of scrap garden hose and siphoning fuel out of our company station wagon—after ingesting a mouthful.

It took me three and a half hours to drive home. I was astonished to finally reach the countryside, and see that every rural arterial road, line and sideroad was clogged with vehicles. It was a bizarre experience to sit in a traffic jam, watching a cow. By the time I reached the village near our home the local propane company tanker truck was driving by. I flagged down the driver, whom I knew. Worried about how much gas was left in our 1,000-litre tanks, I implored if he'd come over and fill them.

"Too late," he said. "Everybody's been asking, and I'm bone empty. And you can forget getting more until the power comes back on."

I made it to our gate, then rolled through the forest down the driveway towards the river, and heard the roar of the generator. My wife came out, looking vastly relieved, saying she was glad I made it home. "It feels like the world is about to change," she said. And it did. The reasons for this event were unclear. The consequences potentially dire. All I could think of was gasoline, money, food, propane. I felt under siege, and yet knew I was far better prepared than most.

With that thought, I hurried back up the hill, to the road, and padlocked the gate.

WASHINGTON AND OTTAWA would spend a lot of money to determine the cause of the blackout which ultimately affected about fifty million people. They found that in just three minutes, beginning at 4:10 pm, twenty-one power plants had shut down. The impact first hit upstate Ohio and New York, and virtually all of Ontario and Michigan. The Power System Outage Task Force report in February 2004, would reveal that a minor power generating plant in Eastlake, Ohio went off-line under peak demand conditions and failed to follow proper protocols. Overloaded power cables sagged, touched trees, shorted and started a cascading effect ultimately shutting down more than a hundred power plants, twenty-two of them nuclear.

In the end, no terrorism, no major systemic failure, no life-altering sequence of events. And the outage could have been far more consequential. It took place in the heat of August, not the deep-freeze of February. It lasted less than a day in most locations, not weeks. Aircraft, subways and street cars were only temporarily idled. Public water supplies in only some cities, like Detroit, were affected. The endless river of transcontinental truck traffic was dammed for less than two days. Most factories were back in production within seven days. The lines, ten deep, for pay phones in Manhattan dissipated within a day. Most urbanites trying to escape the 91-degree heat of New York had to sleep outside only one night. The state of emergency declared in Ontario lasted only less than forty-eight hours.

The event had the effect of paralyzing Canadian and American society in those cities, towns and countryside where the lights went out. It served to remind us that most people no longer carry money, stockpile fuel, have contingency plans, maintain food supplies, have a bad day box or even own a portable radio. Our society's become so complex and advanced that the rugged individualism and self-reliance upon which our modern communities were founded, is gone. The vast majority of Canadians and Americans—like Europeans—have become totally dependent for everyday survival on the proper and continuous functioning of communal systems, managed by governments or large corporations.

Money is one example. Most people today are paid by cheque or direct deposit, and never see the cash. Funds exist only digitally, and are deducted from bank accounts for preauthorized monthly payments, credit card balances or debit card usage. People buy gas and groceries with plastic cards representing money. The transactions are recorded digitally by web-based, point-of-sale terminals and bank computer systems. Millions of us live days, weeks or months on end without the need for actual cash in our pockets. We can even buy our coffees and Timbits with a preloaded merchant point-of-sale card.

So long as all the systems function, the Internet is up, software programs are error-free, operators do not make mistakes, no data centres burn or are flooded, hackers are absent and firewalls hold—and no overgrown trees in Walton Hills, Ohio, touch power lines—then it should all function seamlessly.

But if it does not, then there is no money.

What does this have to do with real estate? Everything. Most of us have invested most of what we have in our houses. As this book attempts to remind, this is a poor decision in times of change, turmoil, economic challenge, market correction, demographic consequences or a shift in investor sentiment. It is also bad planning when environmental degradation or climate change events come crashing into our lives and ripping into property values. It will be even more disastrous in the context of managed collapse, those times when as August 14, 2003 reminded, money, food or an energy source will be more important that granite countertops.

IT SHOULD BE OBVIOUS the world won't remain as we know it. Not even close. The human mantra of endless growth, of expected annual increases in GDP (and endlessly higher real estate values), has created a highly complex society which will break down, because it seeks to conquer and ignore nature. Those overgrown trees in Ohio a few years ago symbolized this well.

But there's no putting climate change back into the bottle. And we're in the age of peak oil, when more than half of all the available, relatively cheap, easy-to-find fossil fuels in the world have been consumed. The rest, experts say, won't last more than a few decades, and consumption is increasing every day—we now consume eighty-six million barrels a day, a quarter from the powderkeg Persian Gulf region. This is the world's primary source of energy and we could lose it at the worst possible moment.

The combination of an energy drought at the very time the world's climate is rapidly changing should be of concern to every real estate investor, unless you plan on cashing out within the next few years. We're now apparently well into an era of extreme weather, changing landscapes and outright threats to some of the most expensive real estate in the world.

In October 2007, the report *U.S. Economic Impacts of Climate Change and the Costs of Inaction* starkly predicted the current American housing crisis is going to get a lot worse, or perhaps never recover, because of what the coming years will bring. It forecasted billions of dollars of damage to infrastructure, a devastation of the agriculture business and higher taxes for everyone, as governments try to cope with rising seas and approaching storms.

Among its predictions were fires in the U.S. West and Northwest due to diminished rain and a melted snow pack; drought and abandoned farms and ranches in the Great Plains; lower water levels and increased shipping costs in the Great Lakes; storm surges and the eating away of pricey real estate along the Atlantic Coast; more drought in the South and in

California where losses will be up to $6 billion a year in the Central Valley alone. In each of these areas, it is conceivable real estate values will drop substantially. In some cases, to zero.

The report also warned of greater health problems for poor and elderly urban dwellers due to scorching summers, widespread crop failures and the soaring costs of food, higher income taxes and fewer government services as politicians try to cope with replacing battered infrastructure, and reduced incomes and job losses. Concurrently, a report on the insurance costs of climate change by European re-insurance giant Swiss Re also warns of the spread of malaria and West Nile Virus as temperatures rise, along with increasing Lyme disease in areas like southern Ontario as ticks proliferate (my dog has already been attacked near our cottage on Lake Erie). It cites the certainty of more asthma, the result of a proliferation of ragweed, stimulated by increasing levels of carbon dioxide.

Some believe some big challenges are already here. Melting polar ice packs have changed oceanic currents, reducing the flow of water around the planet, concentrating more hot water in places like the Gulf of Mexico, and resulting in hurricanes like Katrina turning into hopped-up killers when they pass over the liquid energy. On the Canadian prairies there have been a record number of summer storms, tornadoes, intense rainfalls, wind and hail. In 2007, there were 279 hailstorms causing a record $200 million in crop damage. There were 410 summer weather events in Alberta, Saskatchewan and Manitoba, surpassing the old record of 297. The Canadian Crop Hail Association reported more claims in Alberta than ever before.

One day in August, 2007, Dauphin, Manitoba suffered lightning, torrential rain, high winds and hailstones the size of grapefruits. In June, it rained in Calgary so hard for one hour that the downtown was flooded, and $10 million damage was caused. It was the worst storm in almost a century.

Critics may say these are isolated occurrences, and freaky weather has always been with us. Yet the evidence mounts there are far more such events now, and dire reports on our foreseeable future mount like cordwood.

The 2007 report of the esteemed *Intergovernmental Panel on Climate Change* says that by 2100 seas will be a half-metre higher, hurricanes will be biblical in nature, droughts widespread and a mass human migration take place as temperatures climb by more than two degrees. This, of course, will be gradual—and the process is already taking place. The UN panel estimates warmer oceans and melting ice packs will raise sea levels twenty centimetres by 2050. Each one of those centimeters means the loss of one metre of flat coastal land. And right now, in 2008, 100 million people live within one metre of sea level—which raises the distinct possibility of millions and millions of environmental refugees within the next decade, along with the disappearance of untold acres of real estate.

Already eleven of the past twelve years are among the warmest on record since humans started noting temperatures a century and a half ago. It's estimated that human activity and climate change is resulting in the loss of as many as 147 species of animals a day. Oil is approaching $100 a barrel and political instability is rampant in places—Somalia, Afghanistan, Iraq, Rwanda, Bangladesh, Haiti, Indonesia—where there is environmental devastation such as deforestation, drought and crop failure.

As Jared Diamond writes in his important book *Collapse*, "Today, just as in the past, countries that are environmentally stressed, overpopulated, or both, become at risk of getting politically stressed, and of their governments collapsing. When people are desperate, undernourished, and without hope, they blame their governments, which they see as responsible for or unable to solve their problems. They try to emigrate at any cost. They fight each other over land. They kill each other. They start civil wars. They figure they have nothing to lose, so they become terrorists, or they support or tolerate terrorism."

This climate change, the effects of which are becoming apparent and frightening, occurs at a time when our society has never been more complex, interdependent or fragile. I gave one example—money. Consider another—food. More than 80 per cent of the arable land in North America is used to grow crops which are largely inedible without processing—wheat, barley, soybeans, corn or animal fodder (hay). This agriculture consumes huge quantities of oil in the form of fertilizer, plus lots of energy for irrigated water, since we have depleted soils so badly from their natural state. Then, the raw crops have to be processed into food for a human population to consume, that can no longer can feed itself. In addition, it takes 1,000 tons of water to produce a single ton of grain, and agriculture now consumes 70 per cent of the world's water. Thus, for every calorie of food you eat, ten calories of energy were consumed. It's been estimated the average American meal travels 1,500 miles from field to table. Now, with climate change—vacillating temperatures, eroded soils, uncertain rainfall, devastating storms—agriculture and the human food supply becomes unstable. With peak oil, escalating energy costs and no viable replacement for oil-based agricultural products on the horizon, more instability.

These are the essential elements of an event many refer to as managed collapse. Already 60 per cent of all the energy on the planet is going to support 6.5 billion members of just one species—us. That leaves less than half for the millions of other species that remain, and upon which we depend. Managed collapse means our society is ultimately doomed, and the best that international accords like Kyoto can do is stem emissions of greenhouses gases and slow the inevitable down. This also raises the specter of countries like Canada becoming the destination—willing or otherwise—for millions of environmental refugees, and a transformation of government from provider of social services to our best possible defense against the kind of mass confusion and unpreparedness that the afternoon of August 14, 2003, brought.

Now, you might not have expected the above in a book on real estate investing, but it only makes sense. Coming events will likely change our perception. Housing will once again become shelter, not an investment asset. In many areas of the world, indeed North America and Canada, that's already becoming the case. Houses in regions where the trees are dying, crops won't grow or floods are an endemic will certainly disappoint as investments. Much real estate has become attractive, and valuable, because of where it's located and the climate it affords. Those values will change along with the weather, or the growing incidence of the threat of disease, or the ability to earn a living.

More fundamentally, the potential exists for a gradual managed collapse of the world's most complicated society which will change all priorities. Just as I obsessed about the amount of gas in my propane tanks, the fuel level in my car and the cash in my pocket during the 2003 blackout, so wealth in the near future may be measured in portable commodities, rather than land and buildings. Given even the remote possibility of that by, say, 2015 or 2025, would it not make sense to adopt a long-term plan to shift part of your net worth out of real estate and into cash, or cash equivalents? Financial assets that can be easily liquidated? Or to try and turn your real estate into shelter and sanctuary, as well as an investment?

I was pleased to have a generator five years ago when the lights went out. I'm even more pleased to have one now. But that is just a start.

CHAPTER FIVE

"IT'S A BUYER'S MARKET. THEY SHOULD BE BUYING."

MANIAS INFECT US ALL, at one fevered time or another. In 2000, for example, in the midst of the technology, dot-com, discount brokerage stock market investing frenzy, I launched a net-based broadcasting company, built a TV studio inside a truck, hooked it up wirelessly, parked it in the financial district of Toronto and broadcast live news about the stock market via the Internet eight hours a day. It was the world's first online TV station, and fed an insatiable desire on the part of investors, many of them first-timers, to gorge on hot tips and tales of new millionaires.

In my community and maybe yours, too, it's impossible now to wander into any social event without hearing people eventually talk about their houses. They crow about how much money they've "made" since purchasing, the property values on their street, renovations planned or completed and the landmark prices recently fetched in the area. The buzz, the breathlessness, the wealth effect and the obsession are completely reminiscent of the tech boom. That was when everyone was saying, "it's different this time." This boom would last—since it was based on innovation, technology, progress, advancement, science and the future.

It didn't. And those who had realized big gains on unsold assets saw them eventually melt away in a matter of days. Sellers swamped buyers and prices tumbled. The future would look after itself.

What's the current real estate boom based on? The inherent worth of soil and construction materials? The irreplaceability of land? Timeless architecture? Environmental self-sufficiency? Location? Or is it primarily, as with Nortel shares, mutual funds, gold bullion or tulip bulbs, supply and demand? How is it that one can so easily overwhelm the other, and during an upmarket that so many investors fail to see the tide turning? Surely warning signs would include:

- record-high prices
- record volumes of sales
- record debt among investors
- the decreased ability of new buyers to get in
- public mania

Speaking of such, a tale of two countries seems to be playing out. In the United States, the pro–real estate cocktail chatter is over, replaced with tales of plunging valuations and the faint hope of recovery. In Canada, investors, homeowners and new home buyers continue to be egged on by unqualified statements that prices will continue to rise, and those who snooze will lose. Take the word "house" and replace it with "dot-com," and the comparison is haunting. Consider some recent and telling media reports:

From *USA Today*, January 2008:
"We're really in a danger zone in terms of overall economic activity," says housing economist David Seiders, who sees a 40 per cent chance of recession this year, up from an earlier estimate of 30 per cent.

Mark Zandi, chief economist at Moody's Economy.com, calls the current real estate recession the gravest since World War II. He expects home sales to hit bottom in the first half of this year, with prices continuing to fall until early 2009.

An even more pessimistic economist, David Rosenberg at Merrill Lynch, goes so far as to warn, "Real estate pricing in general can expect to be in the doldrums through 2012."

The biggest problem is the glut of homes for sale—more than 10 months' worth. And about 2 million of those homes (about 2.6 per cent) are vacant, with banks or builders trying to get them off their hands.

From the *Saskatoon Star Phoenix*, same day in January 2008:

The past 12 months have been record-breaking for residential realtors in Saskatoon with 4,446 homes sold . . . sales and average prices are up 45 per cent.

"I guess it might be said that anyone who's out there thinking, 'I'm going to wait to purchase a property because prices are going to come down,' we should encourage them not to think that way," says Henry Janzen, first officer, Saskatoon Region Association of Realtors.

"Now is the time to try and buy," said Kent Bittner, mortgage broker and owner of Dominion Lending Centres on Saskatoon's Wall Street. People trying to enter the market for the first time are concerned they will be left out of the rush, he said, and their worries are valid.

"We do see people, call them first-time homebuyers, caught in the market they know what's going on, they've heard that prices have been increasing. They're fearful that they will be left out in the dark if they don't get into the market soon," Bittner said. "Somebody that's looking right now is best to look seriously in the next couple of months rather than waiting for the passing months, because last year people could easily have paid 30 per cent more just waiting a couple of months."

Bloomberg News, same day, January 2008:
"People do not like to borrow money to buy depreciating assets," says Ian Shepherdson, chief U.S. economist at High Frequency Economics in Valhalla, New York. "Until potential buyers can plausibly believe prices will not fall further, home sales will continue to decline.... When home sales are falling on a national basis, as they are now for the first time since the Great Depression, the real cost of borrowing goes up."

Victoria Times Colonist, Victoria, BC, same day:
The increased value (in municipal assessment, on which property taxes are based) pushed 518 homes past the $1 million mark in 2008. There are now 2,864 Greater Vancouver homes valued at more than $1 million.
"It shows B.C. is a sound place to invest right now," said Rudy Nielsen, CEO of Landcor, a Vancouver-based real estate analysis company.

An anti–real estate mood has swept America. Within months, it will come here. Billions have been lost. Billions more are owed. The damage has been far worse than the fabled NASDAQ technology and dot-com meltdown of almost a decade ago, since real estate ownership is so pervasive.

We made houses too easy to buy, money too cheap to obtain and debt too easy to swallow. Bankers, economists, regulators, realtors, homebuilders, media sycophants and green-eyed investors allowed an asset bubble to be created. As the link between homes values and family income was severed, fools dived in and even greater fools followed them. There will not be a quick recovery—for the reasons outlined in Chapter Four. In fact, real estate values may never repeat in the same fashion.

How black can the mood become? Consider this column, from a December 2007, issue of the *Journal Star*, in Peoria, Illinois:

We're not supposed to have much of a subprime crisis here. So an ad for a real estate auction caught my eye. 'In a buyer's market, YOU should be BUYING!!!' it said. If the stony-faced buyers gathered last Wednesday are any indicator, be glad that Peoria is supposedly doing well.

The auction company will take the top bids to the seller. The minimum has been set. But sometimes the sellers will take less. The first house on his slate has two bedrooms, hardwood floors, one bath and a concrete block garage out back.

'How much? What will you give for it?' auctioneer Joe Cotten cajoles, and the sing-song begins. 'How much? How-much-will you-give-for-it? One hundred thousand dollars? I see smiles. It's a buyer's market.'

A grin flickers here and there, but that is the last of the frivolity. Even for a first-time buyer, even for a rental property, Cotten can't get a bid until he drops the price to $30,000. There is a brief flurry of activity. It stops at $48,000, which is less than the seller's minimum. No sale.

House Two has three bedrooms and one bath, a new roof, siding and windows. Bidding stops at $15,500. 'You can make it up in six months rent!' Cotten pleads. No takers.

House Three has three to 4 bedrooms, a bath and a 2001 furnace. It rented for $525 a month. Bidding starts at $10,000. No one bites. No bids at all.

And so it goes. At the end of the first round of bidding, none of them sells, even at prices less than a good used car. Contacted later, Cotten says he ended up selling 4 of the 17 houses after some haggling in a later round of auctions. He did not think it was appropriate for him to comment much, but this was one of the worst sales he's had in almost 30 years of business. Things have slowed.

'I don't know why people aren't buying. Interest is good. There's plenty to choose from out there,' Cotten muses. 'It's a buyer's market. They should be buying.'

Meanwhile, in Chicago—amid news that resale home transactions across the U.S. were down 20 per cent in late 2007 from a year earlier—appraisers reported the number of days it was taking to sell homes. Houses priced $100,000 to $300,000 took 3 days; homes $300,000 to $500,000 took 130 days; homes $500,000 to $750,000 took 148 days; and homes above that, 194 days. Those were the ones that found buyers. Active (unsold) listings in the city—a larger market than Toronto—averaged 153 days, 175 days, 200 days and 242 days respectively, thus far.

In New York, the *Wall Street Journal* reported the saga of successful securities broker Chris Delzio, who moved to Palm Beach, Florida in 2003, bought two townhomes for less than $100,000 each and flipped them shortly thereafter for double his purchase price. He took the profits, bought land to build five units on.

The nouveau developer built one house on which he spent $203,000, and listed it for sale in a declining market at $210,000. No sale, so the price was whittled down to $175,000. Still no sale. He now rents it for $800 a month, about half of what it costs to carry.

Also in Florida, owners of seventy-nine top-end properties who couldn't find buyers listed them with SKY Sotheby's, a luxury property auctioneer associated with the fine art dealer. Eighteen of them carried no reserve bid, and at the end of the event, they had sold for an average of just 45 per cent of the original asking price. Thirty-five other properties didn't receive a serious opening bid, and went unsold. Commented a story in *Barrons* magazine on the disastrous sale: "(It) certainly said something about the once-torrid Florida luxury-home market…and similar markets around the country. And what it said wasn't reassuring for those with high-priced property to sell."

In Modesto, California, a new home subdivision centred around a street called St. Salazar Circle is in crisis. It is, reported the *Christian Science Monitor*, "the furthest advance of Modesto's housing boom—and the start of its scorched-earth retreat.

Brown, unwatered lawns of foreclosed homes compete with the green grass of neighbours still hanging on. Some of the structures, although new, are missing outdoor equipment like air conditioners, taken by metal thieves. One in four houses in the neighbourhood sits empty.

"Built during the height of the housing boom, they have the newest residents who paid the highest prices with the most exotic mortgages. After seeing prices rise 10 to 20 per cent each year, they're now seeing prices slide downward. 'Right now, our dreams are being crushed,' says Marisol Ramirez, who bought a home on St. Salazar last year for $370,000. Now, it's priced at $300,000 and the Ramirezes are likely to lose it."

Says a local realtor: "There are buyers out there, but they're just not buying. They're sitting on the fence, waiting for prices to drop more. They're going to see it drop and then they'll wait for it to drop some more. They all think it's going to go to zero."

From $200,000 townhouses to $300,000 middle-class homes to $2 million suburban mini-mansions, from New York to Florida to California, the stories carry a common thread. Disappointment and bitterness are expected, along with sadness and investor remorse—but surprise is a dominant emotion. There are millions of Americans, so similar to millions of Canadians, who absolutely did not expect this. As a bankrupt local developer in California asked, "None of the experts saw this drop coming. So why should we listen to them now?"

Why the vitriol at real estate, in the world's greatest housing market? Did investors just expect it to rise forever?

More than anything, there is a sense of betrayal, as the eternal truths surrounding residential real estate are shown to be nothing more than myths. And while a disintegrating market in the U.S.—the inevitable result of overbuilding, speculation, greed, misinformation and mass investor mania—clearly shows this, in Canada there are legions of homeowners for whom reality has yet to dawn.

Here are some myths of Canadian real estate, which have been allowed to masquerade as facts:

Myth #1: Unlike stocks, real estate is a riskless investment

For a variety of reasons, real estate investing is every bit as fraught with risk as putting money into traded securities like stocks, bonds or mutual funds. More so, perhaps.

First, real estate values are dictated (as are stocks) by supply and demand. When one exceeds the other, the price moves. Buyer sentiment can turn negative when the economy weakens, interest rates rise, oil hits $150 a barrel or the nature of a neighbourhood changes—all things sellers can do nothing about.

Second, real estate is extremely leveraged. A homeowner buying with 5 per cent down is leveraging 95 per cent of the value of the property, which means even a minor price fluctuation can wipe out equity. Third, real estate, unlike stocks or mutual funds, cannot be easily converted into cash. In a stock market crash, you can bail out with a single phone call. In a housing crash, you are trapped for months, maybe years, watching values tumble. Fourth, houses costs a bundle to carry, which means you have to get a capital gain just to break even. Stocks, bonds or funds cost nothing to carry, except the interest on any money you borrowed to buy them—and that is 100 per cent tax-deductible. Fifth, read this book more closely. Real estate has just destroyed the financial lives of several million people who thought it was a winning investment. There are regulators looking out for the interests of novice stock investors, and know-your-client rules protecting inexperienced financial market players, but when it comes to getting a mortgage and closing on a house, you're on your own. Compared with Bay Street, Main Street is the true Wild West.

Things sometimes take a hit—even in Calgary

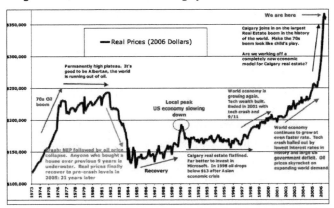

Real estate's boom-and-bust cycle has been experienced at one time or another in many of Canada's major cities, but rarely with more gusto than in Calgary. Riding high on a oil boom in the seventies, real estate took a dive, spent two decades recovering, and then launched into an unprecedented growth phase. Just one thing seems certain—more change.

— www.investingintelligently.com

Myth #2: Houses appreciate

Nothing appreciates on its own without a catalyst. Real estate values, once again, only move in accordance with supply and demand. Resale homes routinely depreciate relative to newly-built ones offering the latest faddish features, and real estate in many places can take a dive based on macroeconomic fundamentals, and stay depressed for years. Real estate also generally rises in inflationary environments, and right now the world is deflating.

That's what happened in Japan, where the market languished for sixteen years after tumbling. In Toronto, it took thirteen years for buyers in 1989 to see average prices recover in pre-inflation dollars, and just recently in inflation-adjusted funds. In Calgary, where the boom-and-bust cycle has been played out several times, homebuyers in the seventies had to wait twenty-one years to see their investments even tread water after oil prices fluctuated. Many believe a similar scenario is gathering today. And, of course, American real estate prices have tumbled since peaking in the last few months of 2005, with more depreciation expected.

It's instructive to remember that no commodity has enjoyed endless appreciation, and every investment boom has ended badly. The people generally hurt the most are the last ones to invest as the market moves into its final up-phase, normally characterized by frenzied sales activity and rapidly escalating prices, and the attitude that "it's different this time." Sadly, it hasn't happened yet.

Myth #3: Canadian lenders are more conservative

We may feel superior to the Americans on many issues—universal health care and no death penalty come to mind—but as far as prudent banking practices and conservative financiers are concerned, forget it. Canadian lenders have been just as "creative" and innovative as their southern counterparts, and with the same potential result—getting people into home ownership who probably have no business being there.

Too many of us believe the American housing meltdown occurred for reasons absent from Canada, namely that millions of financial low-lifes were given mortgages they didn't qualify for to buy houses they could not afford. The real estate experts here point to the fact we have "no subprime market" and therefore are immune.

Wrong. First, the US real estate disaster was not caused by bad lending practices, but rather because the market overheated and melted down due to speculation, overbuilding, greed and panic—all of which are in evidence here. Second, Canadians have no lessons to give to the Yanks when it comes to funny financing. Federally-mandated limits in the United States require down payments for insured mortgages to be 20 per cent of the property's value. In Canada, the limit is just 5 per cent, resulting in 95 per cent mortgages and a lot more instability and risk. In the U.S., the most common mortgage amortization term is thirty years, and in Canada it has recently become forty years. That means borrowers here get lower monthly payments, allowing them to afford more house on the same income. But at the same time this masks the fact they may be spending more than is reasonable or prudent, and it certainly means their total debt to be repaid is massively higher.

Third, there is an active subprime business in Canada, with several of our major banks granting 100 per cent financing to borrowers who have not been able to save any money for a down payment. As already mentioned, our big banks also extend home-buying credit to borrowers who may be self-employed with no ability to prove their own annual income. There's also an active "B" and "C" market for credit-challenged borrowers. And our major banks have become so cavalier about giving money out for residential real estate they don't even bother appraising properties, granting approvals based on just postal codes. Not very conservative—even by American standards.

US lenders, in the wake of the real estate disaster in that country, are scrutinizing not only borrowers but also that commodity their Canadian colleagues are taking for granted—the house. For example, a buyer in St. Paul early in 2008 couldn't close a deal on an $180,000 house, because his bank appraised it as being worth $10,000 less. And US appraisers are now required to disclose if a property is in a "declining market," noting how many listings are on the market, and for how long. Bad neighbourhood? Then cough up a bigger down payment. Except in Canada.

Myth #4: Industry experts are worth heeding
If you believed the bankers, realtors, marketers and economists employed by lenders, you'd think the best time to buy is at any stage of the real estate cycle, and at any

price. The real estate industry is essentially self-regulated, and engages in constant self-dealing. This is regrettable, when the bulk of all family net worth in Canada is in residential real estate.

Real estate experts today are encouraging young couples to buy, when prices have never been higher, warning that they will go higher still. This, despite mounting evidence the economy is poised to soften after almost two decades of advance. Energy prices, climate change, US recession, the credit crunch, lost export and manufacturing jobs. They will have much to answer for.

I was reminded of that one day early in 2008, as oil topped $100, gold hit a record $860 an ounce, political strife tore through Kenya, Pakistan and Afghanistan, freakish weather blanketed the country, the stock market suffered another triple-digit loss and American financial experts were upping the odds of recession. Amid these harbingers of the gathering global storm, RE/MAX Ontario-Atlantic Canada revealed new research on luxury home sales in Toronto, saying they had jumped 37 per cent in the previous months. RE/MAX also changed the definition of a "luxury" home from a property worth $1 million, to $1.5 million, "since million-dollar city homes are no longer the market of distinction they once were."

As media reported the new research, "While a $15,000,000 home would have raised eyebrows a few years ago, that's no longer the case." The real estate industry continually attempts to break the link between income and the ability to purchase houses, to upsell properties, and create the equation between home ownership and wealth accumulation in investors' minds. It may be an effective and clever marketing strategy. It also defines irresponsibility. Real estate has proven to be both a creator and destroyer of wealth. Going forward, I would not recommend owning a $15 million home.

Myth #5: You need someplace to live anyway

Of course you do. Real estate marketers are also fond of saying, "You can't live in a mutual fund," which is equally correct. But real estate as shelter has become hopelessly confused with real estate as an investment asset. Today homeowners expect to live free, since their appreciating home will always be worth more than they paid, when they move on. They also expect rising prices to be normal, and consider decreasing prices to be an unforeseen and cruel financial disaster.

This has transformed home ownership into a short-term financial strategy. It encourages people into a "flip" frame of mind, in which it's perfectly normal to move up to a larger and more expensive home every three years. They expect and count on equity growth to paper over the substantial, real costs of carrying a property, paying commission to sell it and moving. Should the market ever correct, and prices stabilize, let alone decline, they could well end up with a home twice the size they started with, but not a dollar more in equity. They also forget, or are unaware, that the more costly the property, the smaller the universe of potential buyers for it. If the market does slow (inevitable), it's the people in McMansions who take the shortest haircut.

The evolution of real estate from home to investment asset has occurred in most families in a single generation. Many of today's young adults, feeling deprived without their granite and stainless steel kitchens, home theatre rooms, salt water pools and thousands of square feet, grew up with parents who spent three decades in the same small home, raising children, making a life—and becoming free of debt.

Myth #6: A house is a great investment

When it goes up in value. Otherwise, it can turn into a wealth trap. Real estate rises when more people are buyers than sellers, when inflation is increasing the value of most commodities and when investors feel positive about the immediate economic future. Real estate does not climb in value, or fall, when buyers lose faith in job prospects, interest rates rise, the economy stumbles, stock markets lose value, credit becomes more difficult to obtain, deflation strikes or when listings surge and sellers lose their competitive advantage.

History has shown that housing does perform well over decades, countering the effects of inflation and yielding a great tax-advantaged capital gain. Unfortunately, few buyers today hold onto housing for decades, instead treating it as one would stocks or mutual funds.

Myth #7: Better to be an owner than a renter

True enough, if home ownership is done smart—namely, buying an affordable property, paying off the mortgage debt and stabilizing recurring costs. In that way, you know the cost of your locked-in funds. For example, a paid-for home worth $350,000 would actually "cost" the foregone income that amount of money could earn. At a 6 per cent return, it's $21,000 a year, plus property taxes (in Toronto, roughly $3,000), or $2,000 a month.

Could you lease the same property for $24,000 a year? Right now in most regions of the country, the answer is yes. So why would you buy? Because you might expect the home to increase in value, providing you with a capital gain which would offset the lost income on your capital, plus recoup some of your operating expenses. In a rising market, that could well happen. As a long-term investment, a decade or more, the odds of a positive outcome increase. But in a distressed market—the kind likely developing in Canada and already in evidence in the States—the odds shift dramatically in favour of renting.

Consider this media report from Florida, in the *Sun Sentinel*, December 2007:

What a good time it is in South Florida for renters. Rent is falling, and renters have their pick of places to live. An accidental landlord last year would have been called an investor. But now that there are so few home buyers, many investors are renting their homes. The apartment rental professionals say the accidental landlords are a pretty aggressive group, too.

'They're competing with the (apartment) complexes even if that means they only get 50 per cent of what it costs them to own a unit,' said Jack McCabe, of McCabe Research and Consulting, a Deerfield Beach firm that specializes in apartment market research. 'You can rent a $325,000 or $400,000 house for $1,800.'

By comparison, the monthly payment—principal and interest, plus the estimated taxes and insurance—on a $300,000, 30-year mortgage at 6 per cent, would cost you $2,526.

I recalled earlier my own experience as a residential landlord during the real estate downmarket of the early 1990s. A condo unit I acquired in a new building on the Toronto waterfront had a value of approximately $375,000, and the maximum monthly rent I could get for the two-bedroom unit, with balcony, new appliances, a parking spot, concierge and complimentary shuttle bus to the financial core was $1,400. The unit had no financing on it, and yet cost me $1,200 a month in condo maintenance fees, $600 a month in taxes and $200 in insurance. That meant I was $600 a month under water, and had there been a $200,000 mortgage in place, my annual loss would have been close to $30,000, or a negative return of 9 per cent. As it was, with the unit paid for, I was foregoing the income that $375,000 could have generated. My situation became far worse when the tenants moved out—to buy a condo of their own. I knew they were fools, since staying where they were meant a major subsidy by the landlord.

They were far better off being renters, than owners. (I found new tenants I was eventually able to talk into buying the place.)

Myth #8: Rising markets are normal

North America's economy has been a bright spot since the last recession ended in the mid-1990s, expanding in an environment of generally low inflation and cheap interest rates. Technological advance has actually decreased the price of cars and computers, giving consumers a break, while the growth in developing countries was spurred on by the easing of political tensions in the long years following the collapse of Communism.

Of course, there have been financial events—the tech bubble, the dot-com boom and bust, 9/11, the collapse in the cost of money, Y2K, the Asian flu and the War on Terror, for example, but through it all, economic growth continued and real estate values kept pace. Then a housing bubble developed for reasons already detailed, and there's now ample reason to believe its collapse is coinciding with a decline in the economic prospects of the Western world. This is coming at precisely the same time climate change is blowing into all of our lives, along with the realization our Western lifestyle is essentially unjustifiable. In other words, rising markets may be comforting, but they are not sustainable. Assets inflate, investors get stupid, greedy and careless, debt mercilessly accumulates and unforeseen events—like environmental reckoning—create inevitable and sudden consequences. Like the power shutting down that August afternoon in 2003, those who are totally unprepared end up out of gas, out of money and with a dead cell phone on the side of a clogged highway.

A point worth remembering is that a great many people in today's real estate community have never lived through a down market. The last one ended fifteen years ago in most cities. Thus, legions of mortgage brokers, bank loans officers and real estate agents have no experience dealing with a surge in listings, buyer fatigue, panic selling, falling property values, powers of sale and desperately worried, over-extended clients. But, they may be about to learn.

Myth #9: Real estate profits are tax-free

It's accurate that the capital gains Canadians make on the sale of their principal residence is free of capital gains tax. This is held out as one of the major advantages of home ownership, and believed by most to be a significant improvement in the situation faced by Americans.

However, the advantage is tepid, at best, and likely overrated. Of far greater tax benefit is the ability Americans enjoy to write off the interest on mortgages from taxable income, as well as many local and state taxes. They also do enjoy a capital gains tax holiday if they own a property for a specified period of time, and then use the sale proceeds to buy another home.

Why is the Canadian tax advantage overstated? First, the capital gains tax rate is very low. Half of all capital gains are tax-free, and the remaining half of the profit received from selling something for more than you paid is taxed at your marginal rate. For the average person, that would be in the 30 per cent range, which means a 15 per cent tax rate on the overall profit.

But who wants to pay 15 per cent tax on the money your house makes? Actually, most of us already do. That's because the purchase of real estate is subject to a land transfer tax, for example, at the time you buy it. In Ontario, a $450,000 home attracts tax of $5,475 imposed by the province. If your house is in Toronto, then you can add in an extra $4,725, added on by a revenue-starved city in February of 2008. Total, $10,200. Then there are the non-deductible costs of home ownership, including mortgage financing, insurance and utility bills. In addition, property taxes normally cost about 1 per cent of the value of the property each year, and then real estate commissions average 5 per cent or 6 per cent of the total sale price when you unload the property, and are also non-deductible.

Thus, a $450,000 home with a $300,000 mortgage on it, held for five years and sold it for a big profit of $150,000, at a price of $600,000 does not yield the tax-free windfall realtors always speak of. After the land transfer tax ($10,200), five years of non-deductible property tax ($22,500), non-deductible mortgage interest ($114,000) and non-deductible realtor's commission ($36,000), the net loss is more than $32,000, plus insurance, utilities, improvements, maintenance and the income that the down payment of $150,000 might have generated, if invested. A conservative estimate of the net cost of owning that home, which had a "tax-free" profit of $150,000, would be at least $100,000.

Now, imagine selling the home in a declining market, where the $150,000 in capital gain evaporates each month, and yet the taxes and costs and charges remain fixed. Only the commission amount would decline along with your selling price, as the heartache grew.

Myth #10: Canada is different

One of our greatest home-grown real estate myths, relentlessly repeated. Canadian homeowners, fed a steady diet of incomplete and misleading information about conditions south of the border, or in Europe, believe the Canadian market—tiny by global standards—is strong and independent enough to withstand outside influences. This is not the case.

The US housing market overheated and melted down amid a set of conditions remarkably similar to those in this country. Buyers routinely bought more house than they could afford, aided by lenders who extended too much credit, from sellers with inflated expectations or builders flooding the marketplace. Demand dropped as economic conditions weakened and it suddenly became apparent an unsustainable bubble had been created. However, six months before that occurred, everybody was bullish, believing this market would last forever. It did not.

In 2008–9, Canadians face the same conditions Americans do. Oil has never been more expensive, and higher energy costs will affect every family. Credit conditions are tightening across the world, and financing will be harder to obtain for every buyer. The economy is slowing quickly with the expected impact on consumer spending and jobs, and we all face the inevitable consequences of climate change—including higher taxes and a rapid drop in demand for large or energy-inefficient houses.

In addition, Canada faces substantial economic upheaval from the rapid appreciation in 2007 of the Canadian dollar. Gone is the competitive advantage our manufacturers and exporters enjoyed, and the loss of hundreds of thousands of factory jobs has already been one result. On the positive side of the ledger is the impact of record-priced oil on the Alberta economy, where the oil sands will spin off billions in new activity. Tempering that, however, is the environmental impact of this production, which is throwing off more greenhouse gases than any other industry, and creating irreversible landscape pollution in the northern portion of that province. Ottawa has thus far been reluctant to act, as it has been irresponsible in joining the global assault on climate change. This will be an untenable position going forward.

So, is Canada immune, different, special? Or doomed to repeat what we see to the south? What would American real estate investors have done a year or two ago, had they known what was coming? What will you do?

WHEN THE EXECUTIVE director of Canada's national real estate lobby group appeared before the House of Commons finance committee in the late fall of 2007, he brought with him a surprising statement and a disturbing chart. His presentation was predictably upbeat, and his main ask was to allow first-time buyers to gut their retirement plans even more than currently allowed, to find money for down payments.

But during his talk he mentioned the possibility of a "slight decline" in resale home values in 2008. When questioned about that, and the potential devastating impact on new buyers with precious little equity, Pierre Beauchamp quickly reversed course and disowned his freshly-uttered statement. It may have been a truthful and common sense thing to slip out, after all, given the industry Armageddon south of the border, but it would definitely not have furthered his career in the business.

At the same time, though, CREA tabled in its brief a chart showing the average down payment now being made in Canada, as a percentage of the Multiple Listing Service average home price. What had been almost 30 per cent in 1992, had shrunk to just 15 per cent. The implications are significant.

In 2007 more than 521,000 resale homes changed hands, for an average of $312,000. The average down payment was $46,800, and the average financed amount $265,200. That put the average mortgage payment at just under $2,000 a month, requiring an average income of almost $67,000 to carry it—which exceeded the average family income. In other words, the average buyer was totally maxed out. In order to get their hands on a piece of real estate, half a million buyers were willing to take on 85 per cent financing, a number which never before in Canadian history had been so large.

Why would they have such confidence in the future, to pay the highest prices on record for houses, and then shoulder an unheard-of debt load to get them? And why was the real estate lobby group asking Parliament to let first-time homebuyers take up to $40,000 from precious retirement savings to throw at a commodity clearly at the top of its price cycle?

This is the cult of real estate at work, perpetrated by an industry which has drunk its own Kool-Aid far too deeply. Real estate agents are notorious for having portfolios of homes and little else, and of being swept along in the current of every housing tide. The detachment from economic reality rampant in the industry was captured in CREA's year-end forecast, issued about when Mr. Beauchamp hit Parliament Hill.

While millions of Americans were losing their homes and storm clouds gathering over the economy, Canadians looking for direction and investment advice were told:

- Real estate sales will achieve the second-highest level on record in 2008.
- A seller's market will continue "in every province."
- The MLS residential price will set a new record in all provinces in 2008.
- The Canadian market has shrugged off the subprime problems that have been affecting the housing market in the United States. Said CREA president Ann Bosley, a Toronto broker, "The discount off the posted mortgage interest rate may shrink temporarily in response to an increase in the cost of funds for financial institutions, but financing will remain reasonable and supportive of sales activity."

Weeks later, in early 2008, Royal Bank economist Rishi Sondhi told The Canadian Press, "We have a healthy labour market fuelling our consumer spending, our housing market is holding up very well, businesses are continuing to invest at a decent rate."

So, what were young couples in suburban Milton or Kelowna to think? Should they take the plunge, put down what little money they had and buy a new home, with the builder providing 90 per cent or 95 per cent financing? The real estate industry was predicting higher prices throughout the year. The bank economist was sounding positive about the economy. Their parents were supportive and, like everyone else, owned homes. The lenders were eager to give them money, and that granite-and-stainless steel kitchen beckoned.

So, they sign. The house will be ready for occupancy in the Spring of 2009. They can hardly wait.

Back in Ottawa, the federal minister of finance gave an interview in which he sounded as never before. Just seven weeks after he delivered a mini-budget trumpeting a strong economy, record unemployment and government revenues fat enough to finance new billions in tax cuts, he said: "I am worried about the US housing market and what it does to consumer confidence. It's not just subprime, it's much bigger than that."

How big?

A FEW KILOMETRES from my home, as I mentioned, acres and acres of traditional Ontario farmland at the base of the Niagara Escarpment is being scrapped, serviced and turned into subdivisions. Most of the new homes hug the 401 corridor, and the commute by car to the towers of downtown Toronto is about seventy minutes morning and night. By commuter train, forty-five minutes to Union Station.

The homes, as indicated, are constructed on an assembly line in a massive and innovative factory, outside Milton, where workers toil out of the weather for two full shifts a day. Buyers flock to these developments, and the company behind them even runs a "university" for new owners. This corporation, Mattamy Homes, is a major success in the marketplace, has been an outstanding corporate citizen, attempts to build energy-efficient units that buyers adore and has even loaned millions of dollars to the local municipality to help build bigger roads, now that all the old ones are clogged with thousands of new Mattamy residents.

Mattamy gives the young couples what they want. And there seems an endless line of them willing to buy.

In this development, one of the company's many in the Toronto and Ottawa regions, detached homes sit on forty-three-foot lots, and run from $431,990 to $481,990, for houses offering 2,315 to 3,186 square feet of interior space, not counting full basements. Features include granite, marble or quartz kitchen counters, hardwood floors, jetted showers, family rooms with entertainment centres, whirlpool tubs and oak or maple stairs. Of course, there are finished, attached garages, stainless steel appliances, high-efficiency gas furnaces, central air conditioning, landscaped lots and, these days, a complimentary upgrade package.

It's all aimed at first-time buyers—renters, taking the plunge into the ownership of dwellings which their parents, at the same age, probably would have considered mansions. Money is a factor, of course, but apparently not much of an obstacle.

This is how Mattamy's excellent and user-friendly web site handles what it calls, "The Down payment Dilemma."

HOW TO OVERCOME THIS OBSTACLE TO HOMEOWNERSHIP

One of the main things that holds some renters back from buying their first home is coming up with the down payment. The cost of living continues to rise, and in the Greater Toronto Area's healthy housing market, so do home values. It is a wise idea to set saving for a down payment as a priority in order to reap the benefit of homeowner equity. Educated consumers find out what their options are, then do some creative thinking as to how to save money starting today.

YOUR DOWN PAYMENT CHOICES

Depending on how much of a down payment you can afford, here are your mortgage options:

- *Conventional mortgage (25 per cent down payment)*
- *High-ratio mortgage (minimum 5 per cent down)*
- *No down payment mortgage (must have minimum 1.5 per cent value of the home set aside for closing costs)*

High-ratio and no down payment mortgages have lower down payments, but they require a higher mortgage loan insurance premium. This premium is added to the amount you borrow. As a first-time buyer, you can also use money saved in your RSP toward a down payment, with a maximum of $20,000 per person.

The developer also offers some suggestions on how to get a down payment, or at least enough cash for closing costs. They include a second job, borrowing from family, selling possessions and, "take your lunch to work, clip coupons and use them, drive more slowly to avoid unnecessary fuel consumption or take local transit, cut back on long-distance calling."

WHAT'S WRONG WITH THIS PICTURE?

For example, why do young couples need 2,315 to 3,186 square feet of living space, with four bedrooms, three bathrooms, plus at least another thousand feet below grade, and 400 square foot attached garages? Not far from Mattamy's McMansions are the starter homes of another era—built after the last war, which average 800 square feet—still happily occupied. In most of Europe, and in Britain, even new homes routinely average less than 1,000 square feet, and are marketed at families.

When these are "starter" homes now, what on earth do these young buyers aspire to in the future? How can a set of new homeowners ever easily contemplate having a family, when it takes two salaries to maintain and finance this substantial structure? How were such priorities instilled in people in their 20s and 30s, leading them to take on huge debt loads, encouraging extreme financial leveraging, severely restricting their life choices

Take your lunch to work and get this?

A Mattamy-built home being sold in a new development in the west end of the Toronto area. First-time homebuyers looking at spending more than $400,000 are being encouraged to save for a down payment by brown-bagging. Only 1.5 per cent of the purchase price may be required to buy this home.

— Mattamy Homes

and freedom and turning them into indentured custodians of a home large enough for many more people?

What about the environmental impact? While this builder is one of the "greenest" mass developers in the country, offering increased insulation, low-energy windows, heat recovery ventilation unit, sealed ductwork and compact fluorescent lighting, as well as an innovative enhanced energy-savings package, it's still hard to justify a minimum of 1,200 square feet of interior space per occupant, along with a complex plumbing and electrical infrastructure, two baths, three toilets and yards of empty, heated basement space. In addition, every home in this architecturally-designed and integrated community chews up another forty-three feet of land that could grow crops, or stay green and help cleanse the atmosphere. In addition, the taxpayers have spent millions building streets, extending services and erecting new schools—all on land which used to grow corn, market vegetables, hay, cattle and horses.

This, of course, is not the developer's fault or shortcoming. It's that company's mandate to build houses—on land which the local government—keen to expand its tax base—has approved, and to buyers clamouring to live in them. When it comes to endless urban sprawl, there's plenty of blame to go around.

Also disturbing is the new attitude regarding debt. The developer's guide for homeownership speaks about "how much downpayment you can afford" rather than how much house is affordable. The underlying mortgage debt principal is not mentioned because, for many buyers today, it's just not relevant. They don't care if an amortization period is forty years instead of twenty-five, growing the payback amount by hundreds of thousands, because they believe it'll never be repaid. It's all about the carrying costs, not the debt.

In this regard, the line between owning and renting is blurred. Also, there's scant difference, if any, between the discredited subprime lending practices south of the border, and the way Canadians operate. The end goal is home ownership, not financial security or independence—because the very act of owning a home is considered equivalent to financial maturity. At least in Canada. And at least until the kind of economic storm Americans have encountered blows north. Then an eternal truth becomes apparent: Debt is the great leveller.

Also disturbing is the superficial treatment of what the developer rightly calls the "obstacle to homeownership." While generations of Canadians have understood it took years of saving and sacrifice to scrap together a real estate down payment, new buyers are now counselled to brown-bag it, use the phone less and drive slower, in order to gain that big house. Sounding more like the path of ownership to an iPod rather, not a $380,000 home, such advice trivializes and distorts the financial and life commitment at hand.

The picture painted by the marketers of the good suburban life lacks a mention of what happens after closing. In addition to the inevitable blizzard of spending (thank goodness for credit cards) on window coverings, driveway paving stones, area rugs and backyard decks, there are the recurring costs of home ownership—taxes, insurance and utilities—which can easily top $1,000 a month.

What's wrong with this picture? Perhaps plenty. Enough to believe that talking young couples into buying a house with just 1.5 per cent of the purchase price lacks a measure of disclosure. Not, of course, that it takes much convincing. We are real estate smitten. House lusty.

The countervailing argument, though, is simple. And so far, it's been airtight: The relentlessly rising value in real estate wipes out all problems.

People may buy with too little and borrow too much. They may move into grossly more space than they need and live expensive and consumptive lifestyles. They may consume vast amounts of resources. They may end up working just to feed a house, delay having a family and take on massive financial stress. They may likely save not a dime for inevitable decades in retirement. They may contribute to the degradation of our landscape. They may epitomize the over-consumption, inefficiency and selfishness that economist Nicholas Stern warns will doom an entire world and knock us back into the dirty thirties. But, how can you argue when your house makes more money in a year than you do?

One of my friends has a married daughter in her late 20s. She and her husband bought a modest $200,000 row townhouse in Oakville, Ontario with $10,000 down and struggled to hang on. Eighteen months later, in a bubbly market, they sold it for $310,000. After closing costs, they'd leveraged their deposit by a factor of ten. Overjoyed and flush with $100,000 in new-found equity, they bought a large home for $415,000. Their old mortgage of $190,000 has been replaced with one of $315,000. They are delighted. Mom is proud.

The cult of equity is what makes a rising market work. The prospect that your home, whatever its value or location or the amount you put down to get it, will be worth more in a year than it is now, drives yet more buyers to jump on. First-timers are the fuel that keeps the flame burning. Today they're being accommodated by financing innovations which allow for no down payments and lifetime repayment schemes, while being told all it takes is making fewer long-distance calls to jump the bar of home ownership.

Underscoring the social phenomenon is what *Newsweek* magazine's Daniel McGinn described in his 2008 book, *House Lust*. Written during the American real estate orgy which was imploding as he published, it reinforces the fact homes have gone from places of shelter and abode, to investment assets and status symbols now made accessible to all who can ignore debt and fog a mirror enough to qualify for bank financing. Typical of the homebuilding industry during the boom was the comment by one developer, "We're selling extreme-ego, look-at-me types of homes." Between 2000 and 2005, the average house that company constructed rose from 3,200 square feet to 4,800.

Houses, McGinn reports, became substitutes for saving or retirement planning, since everyone believed real estate would be the ultimate storehouse of wealth for the rest of their lives. Owners routinely played houses the way they might have once played stocks. As reviewer Robert J. Samuelson commented, "Sociologically, the 'housing bubble' resembles the preceding 'tech bubble.' When people paid astronomical prices for profitless dot-com stocks, they doubtlessly reassured themselves that they were investing in the very essence of America—the pioneering spirit, the ability to harness new technologies. Exorbitant home prices inspired a similar logic. How could anyone go wrong buying into the American dream? It was easy."

This was especially so in the wake of 9/11. Real estate ownership was patriotism, a reaffirmation in the capitalist spirit that Islamic terrorists were trying to destroy, made all the easier after Alan Greenspan crashed the price of money and opened the floodgates of easy debt.

The conditions were perfect for unleashing one of the greatest asset inflations in modern history. Seemingly unregulated and tacitly welcomed, it became a bubble which would blow far harder and bigger than that of the tech-crazed era, before ending in precisely the same fashion. When it was over, the landscape was littered with losses and debt. Those who saw the danger signs and headed for the exits while the party still raged, retained their new wealth. Those who came late, and bought what the sellers were unloading, were the greater fools.

CHAPTER SIX

"PLEASE BUY MY HOUSE"

IN THE LATE AUTUMN of 2007, my wife was walking our
Siberian around the estate lot subdivision where we'd recently
sold a property for almost exactly what we'd paid for it, two years
earlier. The process had been painful, taking more than seven
months and involving price reductions. Only one other home in
the area had been for sale at the same time. She saw that a SOLD
sign had been pasted over the real estate placard. The owner was
shovelling snow. He saw her, dropped his shovel and came to give
her a hug. They'd rarely spoken. "My God," he said, close to
tears, "it certainly is a buyer's market."

What had happened to him—his home fetching about
$150,000 less than expected and enduring nine months of show-
ings and rejection—was taking place with every property in the
area priced over $600,000. It was also happening in secret. Local
realtors watched the growing imbalance of listings over available
buyers and sat through open houses which nobody attended. In
response they urged their sellers to slash asking prices. Yet the
real estate rot spread quietly and imperceptively, as it had almost
two years earlier in similar upscale American communities.

"I told my parents who wanted to downsize back in early
2006, to sell now, when it was appraised for $1.2 million," a
California blogger posted in December 2007. "So they didn't lis-
ten, and waited one more year, and my dad said I should have

listened to you. They put their home on the market four months ago, and no offers. At the time they listed for 1.2 million, and I told them put it on the market for $900,000, but they said all their neighbours were listing at over a million, and they wouldn't like it. So, now it sits, and they missed the $900,000 mark, so I'm expecting a 'you were right' in about a year, when it sells for $700,000, if that."

A key feature of real estate markets is that they don't get hung with a label until fully mature. So, there's no way of knowing a buyer's market or seller's market exists until it, well, exists. By then it's usually too late to avoid being victimized if you're on the wrong side of the ledger.

Currently, most of us are homeowners. Rates of homeownership in both Canada and the States are at historic levels— approaching 70 per cent. We have never owned so many houses, worth so much, with so much financing and with so much equity at stake. Canadian families have about 85 per cent of their total net worth tied up in residential real estate, and they will be massively impacted if the market decline rotting its way through estate subdivisions in the GTA infects the wider, national community.

It will.

As economist Mike Whitney, of Global Research.ca, put it, there is "a culture of borrowing which has convinced many people that debt equals wealth. It doesn't; the collapse in the housing market will prove how lethal that theory really is."

Whitney continues: "To large extent, the housing bubble has concealed the systematic destruction of America's industrial and manufacturing base. Low interest rates have lulled the public to sleep while millions of high-paying jobs have been outsourced. The rise in housing prices has created the illusion of prosperity but, in truth, we are only selling houses to each other and are not making anything that the rest of the world wants. The $11 trillion that was pumped into the real estate market is probably the greatest waste of capital investment in the nation's history. It hasn't produced a single asset that will add to our collective wealth or industrial competitiveness. It's been a total bust."

Will it be a bust for you?

The fact is, substantial numbers of Canadians currently are engaged in truly risky behaviour. Few voices are being raised in counterpoint. The real estate industry is trying hard to sustain the most profitable boom market it has seen since the end of the Second World War. It attempts to delude an entire population into believing ever-rising housing prices are the norm; that homes can become more expensive even when family incomes stagnate and the economy weakens; that real estate grows in value when all else is devaluing.

Think again. The current boom, which has pushed the price of the average detached home in Vancouver to north of $700,000 and a small home on a 30-foot lot in midtown Toronto to $1 million, can't last. As I explained, the threats of a North American recession, negative demographics, climate change and managed collapse are too significant. Moreover, when first-time buyers are lured into palatial 3,000-square-foot homes with 1.5 per cent down payments and 98.5 per cent mortgages spread over four decades, on Class A farmland, greed has triumphed over reason.

The seeds of the market's collapse have been sown. They are there in the days-on-market statistics (how long a listing takes to sell), the weakening prices of higher-end properties, the new financing which has lowered the bar of home ownership for Canadians, the disconnect between prices and incomes, the paucity of affordable housing and the lack of new, green homes, plus the economic ills taking hold, after more than a decade of advance. Middle-class families have been under intense financial stress trying to juggle the costs of real estate on incomes which have barely budged and tax loads that are still too much a burden.

Now, energy costs are turning ugly. Peak oil, turmoil in the Middle East, the dumping of the Yankee greenback, romping demand from China and other factors guarantee a growing portion of every family's cash will go to gasoline, natural gas and electricity. Food will also get more expensive along with oil. Property taxes will likely increase in those communities which have seen the greatest population growth and are coping with infrastructure deficits. Just look at Toronto's landmark new land transfer and motor vehicle taxes—adding thousands of dollars of cost to legions of families. The transfer tax alone bumps the cost of an average $400,000 home by more than $3,000, adding to affordability woes.

Federal government overspending has fuelled higher inflation, helped augment the loonie on world markets and thus hobbled our exporters and shuttered factories. As a direct result, we are shedding manufacturing and resource jobs, just as the US new housing industry is collapsing and our lumber shipments south tumble. Our big banks have been stung badly, along with financial

Mighty America slides into hock

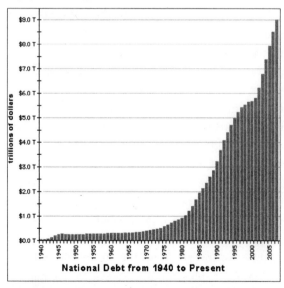

Washington added more than $4 trillion in debt during the second Bush administration, burdened by a costly foreign war, then hit by the real estate crisis. As the US dollar slumped, oil jumped and gold soared. Could this prompt a global depression?
— US National Debt Clock

institutions around the world, as part of the global credit crunch directly resulting from the American real estate market collapse.

Our major client, the world's biggest economy, is not well. Americans have been importing $800 billion more a year than they export, and in just four years after 9/11 added $4 trillion to its external debt. As millions around the world desert the American dollar, it underscores the fear that confidence in that economy is being lost. The Bush administration has spent a stunning amount on the Iraq war—more than $1 trillion, according to the nonpartisan Congressional Budget Office—and for four years embraced a monetary policy of ultra-low rates most economists called irrational. Now some suggest the result will be—when combined with the looming environmental threats—a global depression.

"Virtually nobody foresaw the Great Depression of the 1930s, or the crises which affected Japan and Southeast Asia in the early and late 1990s," says Ambrose Evans-Pritchard, international business editor of the *Daily Telegraph*. "In fact, each downturn was preceded by a period of non-inflationary growth exuberant enough to lead many commentators to suggest that a 'new era' had arrived."

Moody's Investors Service estimates the housing slump to the south of us will last as long as four years. Stock markets in 2008 have been unsteady as investors doubt the ability of global growth to continue, given the threats. Gold prices have raced off the chart as capital around the world looks for a safe place to hide.

In the midst of all this, Canadians are fed a steady media diet of real estate fantasy and bubble market statistics that should cause concern. In early 2008, for example, along with news that sales of million-dollar homes in Edmonton quadrupled came this comment from local RE/MAX realtor Abe Hering that the city's most popular luxury features are now "theatre rooms with terraced seating and $100,000-plus sound systems, fully equipped gyms, quadruple garages, walk-in refrigerators and his-and-hers walk-in closets."

At the same time, a new reality television show was debuting in the United States, joining re-runs of *Flip this House*. Named,

Please Buy My House, the hour-long syndicated program asked desperate, house-imprisoned owners "how far would you go to sell your home?" An early episode included segments on a New England couple with a $1.2 million house that had been on the market more than a year (it sold for $645,000 after they threw in a free designer make-over) and a Florida family unable to sell their home, appraised at $810,000, even when the price dove $150,000 and they used everything from a radio show to massively-planned open house to market it. One scene showed mom and dad and three kids burying a statue of St. Joseph in the yard for good luck because "he's the patron saint of real estate."

What's wrong with this picture? What is it that will protect Canadians from the influences, conditions and financial realities so challenging others? How can a country so dependent on trade with America and so integrated with it, feed off its economic advances and yet escape its reversals?

Ultimately, it cannot. And there's not much question that economic mismanagement in the United States, the age wave in Canada and the climate crisis globally will combine to pressure living standards and make us question Mattamy McMansions, 507-square foot $400,000 Vancouver condos and walk-in fridges in Edmonton.

The denial among homeowners—especially those who paid too much, borrowed too much, or failed to diversify their assets—is palpable. As with the majority of American families in the summer of 2005, we still labour under the impression this bubble market is sustainable, different from all booms which went before, and that price increases may lessen but prices will never fall.

Recently, I received this letter from a young father living in my district:

Mr. Turner, I am aware of the grave threat that climate change, peak oil, the housing bubble and the current global financial meltdown/shake-out pose to Canada. You are one of the only Canadian voices that has been able to articulate the grand picture from 30,000 feet and for that you have earned my applause. The "reality" of North American life is about to change but I feel at a loss as to what I should do to best prepare for or avoid the carnage. I can see the hurricane you are warning of, but feel just as ill prepared as my neighbours who still see blue skies.

As an MP I appreciate that you can't get bogged down in personal advice, but I do hope that you might offer a suggested path for the many constituents who are in my shoes. I live in a townhouse in your riding that I bought with 15 per cent down three years ago (ten year mortgage at 5.15 per cent)...my wife is staying at home to raise our two children. We live modestly and don't over-consume. My gut feeling is to sell the house (and realize the 70K gain), rent for a year or two and then buy back into the market when prices have depressed. My wife thinks I'm crazy....is she right?

I hold your opinion in the highest regard and appreciate any thoughts you might wish to share.

To that, I replied:

Jason, simply, there is only one reasonable course of action, which is to list the house as soon as possible, hope a hungry buyer comes along, and pocket the seventy grand. Go and rent a similar home for (likely) a lower monthly cost, and wait for the inevitable winds to howl through. Odds are the house will be worth less in a year than it is now, and a seller's market will have turned into the same buyer's feast that currently exists to the south.

In fact, you might want to question the whole notion of home ownership for a while. Consider that you face large, non-deductible costs of land transfer tax, mortgage payments, property taxes, utilities, insurance, plus hefty commission when you sell, and the lost earning potential of the money you used as a down payment. The only way to break even if is a substantial capital gain can be realized.

Given all that, you can often improve your cash flow by renting, rather than owning. Plus, if you do own a home and the market turns, you'll find real estate to be an illiquid investment. You can always sell a stock or mutual fund with a single phone call, while it can take months to unload a home, with its value falling every day. In fact, this is already happening in spades to more expensive homes in the region—months on market, and offers for $100,000 or more off the asking price.

By the time your neighbours understand what you have just realized, it will be too late to take action.

Real estate is a fine long-term investment, when you have oodles of equity and the time to watch all kinds of conditions come and go. But for you, go talk to your wife.

I decided to include this letter and my reply as a posting on my online blog, and opened it up for public comments. The reaction was telling. Here's a small sample:

It will be foolhardy to sell one's house because of the things that may happen in the future. Sure, the value of real property may fall, but are you forgetting that you own your house? Don't you think the government will just allow Canadians to just lose their homes just because of the economic downturn? Are you forgetting about cutting down interest rates by the federal government or possible moratorium on housing loans?

If this guy's job is fairly secure, and he can afford his payments, he should stay put. He still has equity (even if some of the equity is initially eroded in the next year). Plus he is young and sometimes the housing market has its ups and downs. He has lots of time to stay the course.

*Why panic! The $70,000 he would realize now, would be gob-
bled up in no time by rent (3+ years); or if he invested, he would
earn about 4.5 per cent in a safe investment vehicle but still have to
pay the $18,000 to $24,000 in his yearly rent. I can't believe that
you, Garth, would giving such an advice. Renting only makes others richer.*

*Renting is simply paying some person's mortgage for them! At
least if this family stays put and rides it out, they are investing in
their own equity every month. Also, you have to consider the personal side of such a move you are encouraging Garth. What if they
have a dog? Are they prepared to give up that pup to move? Very
few rentals allow pets. The kids would have to probably change
schools and give up friends. For me, if I were in his shoes, if possible I'd stay put and ride the wave. As for 'climate change', for me
personally, I think the jury is still out. Sorry, but I won't lay awake
at night because Al Gore thinks I should.*

*The trend will be your friend. The GTA has exploded in growth
because 17 per cent of Canada's population want to live within the
GTA and therefore demand will cushion a long term price decline in
housing. You really have to ask yourself why you live where you live
and whether you like it or not. Renting has its headaches as well.*

*I can't believe that you, Garth, would be giving such an advice.
Renting only makes others richer.*

*Renting means money out the window. While paying mortgage,
most is interest, but some comes off the principle. Whereas rent is
all gone. Not to mention someone still has to pay property taxes,
hydro, gas, water and insurance on a rental, costs which the tenant
pays or the landlord passes on to them. Rent or own, these are still
coming from your pocket.*

*If you take the equity and rent and start digging into this new
found wealth in time you could have very little to show for all your
efforts and be destitute. Real estate (personal residence) is still your
best investment. There is no capital gains on resale. The markets
shifts up and down are historic. I believe if you check the data you
will find that a home has been the best investment over the years.*

You are living in a high demand area of the GTA in a moderately priced home. If the housing market suffers a downturn, you will lose equity, but it will be a paper loss. That is, unless for some reason you absolutely must to sell at the bottom of the market and the home you own goes below its original selling price. If (and it's a big if) that's what you see happening then by all means sell but if not, I'd buy myself some stability, a neighbourhood and some pride of ownership and stay put.

Most likely all you stand to lose is some paper money and where you are, if you wait a few years, you'll earn it all back. And, what if you guess wrong? Can you live with those consequences? Can you gamble on your family?

Give me a break. I've lived on this planet long enough. Nobody, but nobody, can predict the future, particularly the housing market in an highly desirable, high growth area. Sorry, the pressures on the housing market in Revelstoke, BC (a lovely area, if one likes mountains, BTW) will never be the same as that which is experienced in the GTA. In the end, we all have to live somewhere and it may as well be in a place that we own.

I sold my house in 1989 and was what Garth would call lucky to get out. Now it's worth double what I paid for it and I would have paid off my mortgage. I was never able to get back into the market and I'm still renting. Real estate is a long term investment. If I was you, I'd hold on especially with a ten year mortgage at low rates. It's a forced saving plan and even if it's only worth what you paid for it, in twenty-five years you own it. In twenty-five years, as a renter, you'll still be renting.

The cult of real estate is intense, maybe overwhelming. A majority of us will be incredulous when homes no longer sell, and average prices fall. Substantial numbers of owners today have never lived through a falling market, and can't imagine one. None of us have experienced a climate change crisis, or the economic challenges, weather events and higher taxes that might bring. Likewise, we may be witnessing the migration of economic power from West to East—not necessarily a positive thing for Canada. Or the ending of a hundred-year era of cheap-oil prosperity. And never before has any Canadian lived through the mass arrival at retirement age of nine million taxpayers.

The consequences could be long-lasting and profound. They might be mitigated by other opportunities—new energy generators, new technologies, new sources of economic growth, a successful global strategy to stabilize the environment. Hopefully so, in which case the real estate hit will be short-lived.

But a hit is coming. Are you ready?

GIVEN THE ABOVE, HEREWITH SOME STRATEGIES:

(A) HOMEOWNERS

Most surprised by future events will be those who already own real estate, believe in it, have stowed most of their wealth there, and been reassured by the industry the inevitable trajectory is up. In declining markets, some real estate remains fairly buoyant, some stays saleable, and a lot goes toxic. As markets change, timing is also critical, since momentum is established by word-of-mouth, then by the media. Finally, as real estate migrates from being desirable to destructive, debt and cash flow turn into major issues, especially for those with little equity or the capacity to withstand a financial hit. The worst thing these homeowners can do is hang on and wait for things to improve. The current American real estate collapse is forecast to drag on for four years from start (2006) to recovery, but could endure far longer given the changes described above.

Homeowners should remember that people who bought houses in 1989 in Toronto had to wait thirteen years to come up for air, while owners in Calgary who were caught in an oil-induced market correction stayed under water for two decades. Given the long-term threats we now face—unknown in previous market dives—the period of uncertainty and losses could be long indeed.

Some choices:

- Wait and see what happens. Try to time the moment when the market turns, selling at a profit, to a greater fool.
- Hang on to real estate and hope for the best—a downturn of just a few years.
- Liquidate now, invest the proceeds, and rent.
- Sell with a long close, hope the contract is honoured, then buy back into a declining, buyer's market.
- Ignore it all.
- Diversity, and promise yourself never to be so foolish again.

Other actions that seem prudent at this time.

BE RID OF HOUSING THAT HAS A DIM FUTURE.

If the United States experience is a guide, and it should be, large, expensive homes are taking the greatest hit in valuation and suffering the worst drought of buyers. Real estate deflation has a history of attacking the wealthy first—as also happened during the 1930s when much so-called luxury housing became obsolete, seen as a giant drag on wealth. Eventually a great deal of it was converted into apartments or multiple owner-occupied units.

When times are tougher and credit harder to find, the appetite for luxury fades fast. Not only do fat houses cost a lot more to

Those unloved McMansions

Rising energy costs, higher property taxes and a chill on financing have helped scare buyers off, and ravage resale values.

buy, they are far more expensive to own, with higher utility, insurance and property tax bills. Expect this to get worse. With oil at record levels, home heating bills will rise substantially, while declining property values will likely encourage municipalities to jump mill rates.

As the population ages and the boomers inevitably downsize, expect a glut of four-bedroom, pool-afflicted, suburban homes to hit the market, deepening and accelerating the real estate melt. Mostly energy-inefficient, in areas devoid of mass public transit, they will attract precious little interest, despite plunging valuations. The situation will only worsen as environmental concerns, and soaring energy costs, turn these boomer castles into unwanted piles of used building materials.

GOT ONE? SELL IT.

In fact, selling's a good option now for anyone with unrealized capital gains.

If the coming market downturn is short, you might be able to retrieve that windfall in a few years—and suffer only the loss of income the money might have provided. But if things unravel, as seems more likely, you may have to kiss the cash goodbye if you don't get it into your pocket now.

Of course, selling is not easy or simple or cheap. It involves giant personal disruption, not just in the event of a move, but also in the listing and showing process. In a competitive market where every potential buyer is godly, your home must be ready for an inspection at any time—cleaned, neat, beds made, dishes away, dog absent. You need to find an aggressive, competent, experienced agent with a good track record in your area and an extensive marketing plan. You must accept every viewing, and make the home available at almost all times.

Be ready to throw in all your appliances, be flexible on the closing date, agree to a home inspection and then be prepared to correct the faults it might discover. In a buyer's market, you do whatever you must to get a signed offer. And, above all, ensure you receive the largest possible downpayment and a stipulation that, in the event of a buyer default, the money is not returned. In a declining market, you may find a buyer getting cold feet as prices tumble, or believing he can bolt before closing, then come back and save $20,000 or so with a new offer—which you'll be desperate enough to take. And chances are you will.

Most Canadian homeowners, save those who purchased in the last few months, have made money on their houses in the frothy bull market. This capital gain can be realized tax-free, as previously mentioned, because it comes from the sale of your personal residence. Since most families have the bulk of their net worth in their home, this gain's of huge importance—it represents the only return on the large investment they've made. So, because they have gambled on a single asset, and been so dangerously undiversified, why gamble again and risk losing it in a falling market?

Sadly, many will. Most Canadians, in fact, will take this chance. Some will deem the hassle of listing, selling and moving too much trouble. The majority will be in denial, choosing to believe the real estate industry when it says a market downturn is nothing more than a temporary buying opportunity. They're part of the cult who believe it's different this time, that the price of an asset class can rise forever, and history will be made.

But what if it's not? The owners of $800,000 homes, now languishing on the market for $600,000 or less in Florida and California—where prices were steaming in 2005—certainly wish they'd taken quicker action. By waiting just a few months, even weeks, they became part of a market in which a rising tide of listings swamped a shrinking pool of buyers.

In many cases, the owners of expensive, top-level homes suffer the most, even when they are newly-constructed, energy-wise and well-located gems. Why? Simply because potential buyers of those properties are existing homeowners themselves, who must find buyers for their own real estate before they can move on. In tough times, the dominoes line up quickly as capital is frozen solid within the walls of houses that cannot find takers.

Expensive home. Long months questing a buyer. Lowball offer. No choice. Heartbreak.

There seems no question the economy in the next few years will be changed, more difficult. The threats we face, which have been mentioned here, are tangible and large. It's hard to imagine how the impact on real estate, of economic slowdown, demographics or a climate crisis will be positive. It's difficult to understand how, with homeownership levels running at almost three-quarters of the population, and a million newly-built homes being added in Canada in the last five years, how owners think they can become sellers at the precise moment of their choosing.

Those days are closing. If you need the gains your house has made, realize them now. If this is money you have counted on having, then take steps to get it. If your family needs this capital to meet its goals—university tuition for children, retirement nest egg for you or funds to pay for the care of aging parents—then why would you gamble on the future by not cashing in?

Of course, some will argue sellers face another gamble—that by exiting now, they might be forced to buy back into a rising market. That's certainly possible. But is it likely? The historic relationship between home prices and income has been broken, and to restore it, prices must fall or incomes rise. Even if we were not facing tough economic times in an uncertain world, is there a reason families would start seeing substantial wage gains, deep new tax cuts or a dramatic drop in interest rates?

The odds of that are slim. The likelihood of a real estate tumble, large.

BE REALISTIC.

Smart sellers will realize that in most markets, in all but some select neighbourhoods, the bidding wars are over. Multiple offers will be a memory. Buyers lined up in six cars at the curb will vanish. The number of showings will plunge over the course of the next couple of years. Agents will spend a bundle advertising, without apparent success. Open houses will be lonely. Those people who do show up will more often be looking for decorating ideas than new digs.

When potential buyers have such choice, their attention turns to just one thing: Price. If a property does not sell in a reasonable period of time—now measured in a month or two, not days or weeks—they it's on at the wrong price. Experienced agents will understand this, and suggest a reduction. Do it. With what's likely to come, there is nothing more important to your financial health than a quick sale.

One major mistake is to list initially at the wrong price. Occasionally agents hungry for a listing will sign you up with an assurance they can find a buyer ready to pay what you think your home is worth. Unrelentingly, homeowners believe the highest sale price in their area is the base value of their home. Agents offering a "free appraisal" may also give you an inflated idea of the market value of the home in order to get some business.

Going to market at the wrong price usually, and ironically, means you'll sell for less than your property's worth. That's because an expensive listing will quickly get stale, lose the interest of both agents and buyers, and languish until the price is dropped. Interest and excitement will not return until the real estate looks like a bargain, at which point you can expect a low-ball offer from a sharp buyer who understands that months on the markets means seller desperation. If you turn it down, it could be months more, and further price reductions, before anther one materializes. Can you afford that?

Remember that the real estate market is not really so different from the stock market. An asset is worth what it's worth at the time it's offered for sale. That value is ascribed by the market-place itself, dictated by demand for what's being offered. Nobody cares what you paid for it or how you feel about it.

MAKE IT PERFECTION

In a buyer's market, which will describe the years before us, the number of active listings will soar, at least for an initial period before many potential sellers give up. There will always be people who need to move on, need to chase jobs, need to retire or seriously need to tap into the wealth they've buried in their homes. Thus, these folks are in competition with each other to sell, and that makes the buyers supreme.

In such times, the house you're offering stands a better chance of success the more perfect it is. Buyers who can afford to be choosey, will be. Expect any sale to be conditional on a professional home inspection—a three-to-six hour process which will tell the buyer the state of the furnace, plumbing, roof, electrical system and appliances. Every tap and outlet will be checked, along with the basement for signs of insects, pests, mould, rot or even slight dampness. When the report is in, a seller can also expect the buyer not to firm up the conditional sale, and sign that precious waiver, until the price is reduced to compensate for deficiencies, or the problems are repaired.

A good agent will also guide the seller through the staging of the home. Don't be shy about repainting, redecorating and ridding it of clutter and surplus furniture. In a buyer's market, this is a beauty contest. Curb appeal and first impressions are huge. So is Internet marketing, since it's now estimated nine out of ten buyers do their initial cull of potential properties online. It's a good idea to spend some money on this yourself, unless the agent is very net-adroit. Establish a separate web site for your home, with tons of pictures, descriptions, views of the neighbourhood and attributes—then aggressively market the link on blogs and real estate forums, and in your agent's traditional ads.

Suppress the urge to renovate in order to sell. You will never get 100 per cent of your investment back, since buyers invariably want to make a home reflect their own tastes. Even updating kitchens and bathrooms is a waste of time—you are far better off just to chop the asking price to the point where a buyer is able to do this work himself, adding the cost to the new mortgage. Remember that in a buyer's market, it's all about price—and everything you do will be discounted.

If you want to spend some useful money, there are only two ways to do so. (1) Paint the interior, and (2) improve the exterior—flowers, trees, shrubs, a stone walkway and trim paint are well worth the money.

Selling in a buyer's market is a shocking experience for those who bought when times were buoyant and houses sought after. I've purchased real estate when making a bid conditional even on a home inspection was out of the question—when it was necessary to view the home for the first time with an inspector in tow, then rush back and write the offer. In rising markets with the spectre of multiple bids and sustained buyer interest, sellers can afford to hold out for their price, to ignore imperfections and deficiencies in the house and to reject any offer which isn't clean.

For a huge number of homeowners today, this is exactly the environment in which they bought. They're conditioned to believe homes rise in value continuously, and an army of willing buyers waits around the corner. Many of them are also financially stressed by their real estate, since they jumped in with small downpayments and large mortgages. They may believe it's impossible to get out for substantially less than they put in.

Some advice: Given what's ahead, waiting is no strategy.

THE CASE FOR RENTERS

For many of us, the biggest obstacle to selling real estate and unlocking the much-needed wealth it contains is the belief we'll be homeless. The housing lobby's done a bang-up job at convincing Canadians that owning a home is the only sound living strategy, and that people rent only when they're impoverished, newly divorced, going to university, financially stressed, can't get a mortgage or socially unstable.

This is bizarre, given the true costs of home ownership, and when the object of being alive is to enjoy a well-financed and varied life. As I detailed earlier, I've been a landlord who actually envied the tenants I subsidized each month. In both residential and commercial properties, I've borne substantial costs and responsibilities as an owner that the renters were shielded from. Even if they stopped paying me rent, it was impossible to remove a tenant (in the case of the residential property) or to force compensation, without months of legal wrangling and thousands of dollars in fees.

I've also been an owner of dozens of houses, and the tenant of several. In all cases, day-to-day life was no different. In fact, when leasing, I have the option of calling the landlord for relief in the case of a basement flood, balky refrigerator or irritated air conditioner—problems which, as an owner, would take big bucks and more than a single phone conversation to solve.

Interestingly enough and despite the real estate binge we've all been on, a majority of people in cities like Toronto, New York and Los Angeles rent, instead of own. In L.A., for example, it costs homeowners an average of about $2,000 a month to finance their places (not taking into account the zero return on the capital in their houses), while the burden on the average renter is half that amount.

In Toronto, with more than 55,000 condo units in various stages of construction at the end of 2007, one of the certainties going forward is a huge selection of spanking new, state-of-the-art rental units, and steadily declining rents. This is because an estimated 40 per cent of those units were bought at pre-construction offerings by investors with absolutely no intention of ever living in them. As the boom housing market turns to bust, it will be impossible for most of those smart owners to sell, meaning they'll be highly motivated to rent at almost any rate, in order to mitigate operating losses. A reluctant landlord used to be called an investor.

In fact, it's already starting. A month's free rent, complimentary parking spot and bonus health club membership are some of the incentives being thrown tenants' way in what has quickly turned into a renter's market in the GTA. Be certain this will continue, as thousands of new condos and townhouses come to market, owned by people who have absolutely no option but to lease them out for whatever they can get.

By the way, condo living has its charms, in case you haven't tried it lately. Since I am in Ottawa often, I maintain a two-bedroom condo in that city, in the downtown core, a five-minute walk from Parliament Hill. The building is reputedly the region's best, with concierge, reserved parking, health club, business facilities, high-level security, upscale finishes with oodles of marble, granite and hardwood. Units there sell for between $600,000 and $1.5 million. Dogs are welcome, so when I'm on duty in the House of Commons, wife and Siberian travel with me.

I'd never sink that kind of money into a business-related pad, but because I rent, I get to enjoy that lifestyle while the owner-investor pays the bills. Consider his situation: At $600,000, with a $100,000 down, the condo's mortgage would cost about $25,000 a year, plus condo fees and property taxes of at least a $1,000 a month. Add to that the lost earnings on the down payment, which at a modest 6 per cent would be $6,000 more. In other words, it costs the investor well over $40,000 a year to own my apartment, and yet I pay just a fraction of that.

What's more, thanks to provincial laws establishing tenant's rights, when the lease expires, it automatically becomes a monthly contract, with exactly the same protection as if the lease were still in force. I can be forced to leave only in the instance of the landlord himself, or his family, proving his intention to occupy the unit.

So, why would I own such a unit? Only if I believed a capital gain on the condo was possible, large enough to pave over annual expenses of $40,000—minus real estate commission. The chances of that going forward, are likely nil. The unit would have to sell after three years for north of $750,000, and if not owner-occupied, the investor would still be under water since capital gains tax on $150,000 would be payable. Ouch. So, what was the investor thinking? He's losing more than $10,000 a year on a piece of real estate which he may be lucky to sell for what he paid. The only saving grace for him is that the loss is deductible against other income. The real benefit goes to the tenant.

But such a sweet deal is not just for condo-dwellers. Likewise, the stock of rental single-detached housing on the market is steadily swelling, and the lease rates are actually declining.

Thus, I'd argue that if you share my fear of a real estate melt in the coming years, an excellent strategy is to cash out of your principal residence and lease a home until the housing storm has passed—or at least until the future is more certain. At that point, the opportunistic and the brave can buy back in, hopefully at realistic prices. Those who disagree, like the many people I quoted above who posted to my blog, have arguments more rooted in myth and emotion than fact. For example, *"I can't believe that you, Garth, would be giving such an advice. Renting only makes others richer. Renting means money out the window. While paying mortgage, most is interest, but some comes of the principle. Whereas rent is all gone."*

First, my Ottawa rent is hardly making my landlord rich. Second, as an investor with tenants, I've personally experienced just how much these clients end up being subsidized, since their costs are fixed while the owner has to shoulder rising property taxes, insurance charges, uncertain maintenance costs and financing charges. Third, in a world of forty-year amortizations, it's tough to see the difference between leasing and owning, when mortgage payments equal a direct transfer of wealth from homeowner to banker.

This is because the longer the payback period on a home loan, the greater the interest bill, the larger the total amount to be repaid and the more glacial the buildup of owner equity. For example, a $300,000 mortgage with a forty-year amortization, borrowed at 7 per cent will cost the homeowner (as mentioned in Chapter Two) over $584,400 in interest, and $884,400 in total. That is a staggering way to borrow money, and a very expensive trade off for a lower monthly carrying cost. But how does this compare with renting?

The mortgage payments total just over $23,000 a year, of which more than $20,000 is interest. The amount of debt being retired each month, and the corresponding growth in equity, is $289. After five years, the homeowner has shelled out more than $115,000 in mortgage payments, of which over $100,000 was interest. If the home were sold at the end of five years, the owner would still owe the bank $280,011—which means the "smart" real estate investor spent a hundred thousand dollars to rent $280,000 for sixty months.

Tell me again how this is more logical than renting?

So, obviously, those criticizing renters who eschew owning for a while fail to realize the true costs of hanging on to a house, especially in a declining market. Let's take a $400,000 bungalow in Toronto, which currently leases for $2,500 a month, plus utilities. The person buying it with $100,000 down and the $300,000 mortgage exampled above would have mortgage costs of $1,900, property taxes of $500 a month and insurance costs of $200. Monthly total—$2,600. Plus there's the $100,000 invested in the home, which could earn 6 per cent invested in a portfolio of safe securities, or $500 a month, bringing the cost of ownership to $3,100. In addition, there are renovation and maintenance costs. In this case, the loss of $600 a month, or $7,200 a year. There is only one reason why anyone would want to do this, and that is the potential of a capital gain brought about by a rising housing market.

If you believe that market will continue to advance, then buy, sustain the operating loss and hope you're right. If not, rent. Five years from now you'll have saved $36,000 and may well be able to buy the home for a great price from an exasperated and jaded owner, dismayed at $36,000 in losses. I wouldn't even be surprised to see him pay the closing costs—thankful he has a willing buyer and can avoid the hefty sales commission.

Also be aware that what was a seller's market in real estate, which turned into a buyer's market is about to evolve into a renter's market. Asking rents have already started to plunge, and will be one of the defining features of the landscape going forward. With tens of thousands of new condo units coming on to the market in Toronto, with the coming inability of thousands more owners to find buyers for their properties in Calgary, Edmonton or Montreal, there will be intense competition for tenants. Today's average rents have only one direction in which to travel.

(B) HOMEBUYERS

As the market turns, buyers emerge as the winners. Suddenly the same amount of money delivers a lot more house. In just weeks or months, a sea of new listings flows onto local markets, giving buyers choice. Most importantly, competition erupts among sellers, not buyers, and each month that overall sales stagnate, that prices flatline and then decline, that competition intensifies.

In a seller's market it's possible to offer what you feel like paying, instead of what the vendor is asking. You can be a vulture investor. You can make an offer conditional upon securing what you want, or what protects your interests. Make it conditional upon the sale of another house, or being approved for financing or a successful home inspection. In a seller's market you can even ask for vendor take-back financing, to secure a better interest rate, at least for a year or two. You can demand the appliances, the window coverings, the lawn tractor, or have the vendor pay your closing costs, including land transfer charges. You can dictate when the deal will close, making it most convenient for you, and secure a deal with a minimal down payment.

The seller, and the seller's agent, may squawk, but to no avail. In a seller's market there's always another house—or twenty— with as many vendors desperate to get an offer.

This, in other words, is about as much fun as you can have in real estate. Consider it buyer's revenge—payback time for those multiple-offer bidding wars in which a vendor created an auction for a property you never actually had the time or opportunity to properly research. In this situation, you can be methodical and meticulous, maximizing value and minimizing risk.

Already this is becoming the case, particularly in the large Eastern Canadian centres. A year ago it was impossible to buy with a clause giving you three or five days to have the home inspected, and now it's de rigeur. Buyers are also demanding, and getting, defects repaired, sales conditional on financing and even a new paint job—as well as substantial price reductions at the top end of the market.

As conditions weaken, the economy wobbles, the financial pages fill up with dire headlines and politicians tell Canadians to tighten their belts, price restraint will hit every part of the market, and every region—even the booming western cities of Calgary, Edmonton, Kelowna and Vancouver. In fact, sellers in those places would be wise to reflect on what happened in those areas of the US (California, Nevada, Arizona, Florida) which experienced the greatest price inflation during the housing bubble. Today they're states of broken dreams and homeowners thirsting for offers of any kind.

In short, if you've got financing, the time to buy houses approaches. Real estate will always have a future, and can always build wealth—like most other commodities. Just ensure you act at the right moment, in the right location and, especially, on the right property.

The big guys know this. A whopping 2008 sale of 11,000 properties in eight states by America's biggest homebuilder, Lennar Corp., set a new record low for prices—forty cents on the dollar. Morgan Stanley Real Estate paid that much—60 per cent off the appraised value—for homes in thirty-two communities.

"Vulture" investment funds have sprung up across the States, taking advantage of desperate sellers. As one opportunist told Bloomberg News, of his favourite area, "If you're a vulture, Florida has more carrion. This stuff is lying on the ground. It's lost life. Some of the stuff in Phoenix is still breathing. Perhaps not for long."

Hungry? Here are some other things to consider, as our market slides.

BUY REAL ESTATE WITH A FUTURE.

Two factors will heavily influence real estate in the next decade and determine which properties maintain or increase in worth, and which stagnate and devalue. They are the age wave and the climate.

Buyers should first realize that Canada—like the United States—has seriously overbuilt. We have been throwing up new houses at an annual rate of 220,000 or greater for the past number of years. This means that about 1.2 million new homes have been constructed since 2003 and added to the national housing stock. By comparison, new housing starts in the United States in late 2007 were running at the level of 1.1 million a year, off more than 20 per cent from previously, and at the lowest point since 1991. Given that the US has a population ten times our size, our developers were actually building two homes here for every one there, relative to the potential number of home buyers.

(Housing starts in 2007, by the way, chimed in at almost 230,000, the second-highest level in twenty years. Said Canada Mortgage and Housing Corp. economist Bob Dugan in early 2008, "Growth in housing starts was driven by low mortgage rates, solid employment, income growth and a high level of consumer confidence." It will be changes in three of these four factors which so alters the situation in years to come.)

As 2008 dawned, there were more than two million newly-constructed, never-before-lived-in houses for sale in the U.S., and another four million-plus resales on the market, many of them built in the last few years. Collectively, we've clearly been on a construction orgy in North America, with the result being overbuilding that can only be sustained by a real estate bubble in which more and more renters become owners, thanks to cheap financing and strained judgment. In the States, the party is over and new home construction has ground to a halt. Can the future hold much different here?

Expect a great deal of this existing house stock to sell for pennies on the dollar because it just isn't what people will want. As I said, buy real estate with a future—appealing to downsizing boomers and everyone freaked out about runaway energy costs.

SIZE MATTERS

One of the nasty surprises awaiting recent buyers of those 3,500-square-foot suburban granitized, stainless palaces on their own patch of former farmer's field near my house could be a decided lack of buyers when they come to bail. Those four-bedroom, three-bath, double-car garage homes may be packed full of creature comforts and very well-built, but for a coming wave of real estate buyers, they're just too big, too remote and too much to consider.

Ditto for the aging, multi-bedroom behemoths of the 1980s, of which there are millions. These could be the orphan properties of the immediate future, unloved, unwanted, expensive-to-maintain houses with backyard pools hungry for their chemical fix, more bedrooms than there are Canadians and located on crescents, cul-de-sacs and thoroughfares lacking public transit, points of social contact or even a neighbourhood convenience store. This is the kind of real estate that car-cultured baby boomers once aspired to, but will inevitably be dumping. If they can.

Real estate with a future

Aging baby boomers could be seeing houses like this, in Guelph's Arboretum project, as hot properties. Under 2,000 square feet and in the $300,000 range, it caters to a large and growing market.
— Reid Homes, Village by the Arboretum

Will these millions of near-retirees be looking to trade their old suburban oversized homes for updated versions further removed from downtowns, shopping, hospitals, transit and a quart of milk? Hardly. Just the opposite.

For reasons of both aging and the environment, less will be more going forward. Empty-nester boomer couples will be looking to downsize into units—bungalows, townhomes, condo apartments—of 750 to 1,500 square feet. Less infrastructure to break down, lower maintenance and energy costs, cheaper property tax bills, lower capital costs and far easier to live in, with creaky knees. Besides size, price also matters, since a majority of boomers—without corporate pensions—need to liberate capital from existing homes and will be loath to tie as much up once again in a new home, with questionable resale value.

The third key ingredient for this downsizing crowd is location. Some boomers, unable to shed their hippie roots, and finally free of the tedium of daily work, will head for the country, where they can grow lambs and carrots. But the majority will likely migrate into urban settings, and for sound reasons. Access to theatres and restaurants and upscale shopping is part of the motivation, along with proximity to medical specialists. Also pushing the decision will be the extreme cost of fuel, and driving in the next decade, as gasoline soars, automakers are forced to comply with stringent, expensive regulations and as a new generation of low-speed and limited-range electric vehicles bursts onto the roadways. Suited far more to city boulevards than 400-series highways, they'll provide another reason city living is the preferred choice.

For this reason, one of the real estate bright spots in the next few years will be urban condos of livable size (no lofts, no 500-square-foot micro pads), city bungalows, towns and some duplexes. In fact, prices of such units may stabilize or even increase while the rest of the market languishes, as empty-nesters and first-timers duke it out.

Another place where the boomers will have some positive influence is in retirement communities—but not the cheap-at-all-costs deserted former mining towns of northern Ontario which are trying to pass themselves off as frozen meccas for seniors. Rather, our future retirees will be more interested in well-equipped homes in more central locations that offer completely independent living and the kinds of houses which retain their value for resale.

An example is the "Arboretum" project in Guelph, a city of 80,000 an hour from Toronto, where acres of architecturally-designed bungalows of less than 2,000 square feet are clustered within the city limits, around a community complex with shopping, pool and concert hall. Set up as a life-lease condo community, there is no outside maintenance to be done, with monthly fees in the $500 range, taxes of $3,000 a year, and prices in the mid-three hundreds for two-bedroom houses.

An obvious conclusion: Buy real estate with a fighting chance of retaining its resale value. Consider size, maintenance costs, location, livability and the demographic pool of future buyers. Reject houses which were born of another time—too big, too much space to heat, too many empty bedrooms, too suburban, too remote, too car-centric, too lonely, too much hydro and gas, too much property tax and too much infrastructure. Pools, pool houses, hot tubs, triple-car garages, media rooms, rec rooms— bad. New windows, heat pump, veggie patch, clothes line, generator—good.

Buy what has a future, and above all...

THINK CLIMATE

Demographic pressures will combine with environmental panic to redefine what it is in real estate that people want, won't hesitate to buy, and even spend more money to get. In the next years, nothing will motivate buyers more than slashing energy costs and feeling prepared for the climate storm to come. Having a non-green, energy-sucking house will be akin to the way we now feel about smokers. They'll be shunned, discriminated against and devalued.

Already, just at the edge of the climate-dominated years to come, home seekers are indicating a strong preference for houses they consider green. A late 2007 survey by Royal LePage found 72 per cent of Canadians said they would look first for a home with green features, and more than 60 per cent told pollsters they'd actually pay more for it—up to a premium of $20,000. Soon, it will be green at any costs, as people understand that a third of all greenhouse gas emissions come from buildings, and as tight, energy-efficient homes become both sanctuary and status symbol.

The cost of maintaining a home will be far more of a motivator than it is today. Hydro, home heating oil and natural gas costs could easily double or triple going forward, the result of serious government attempts to curb consumption through taxes and levies, and the simple fact we have reached peak oil, and are now on the declining side of global oil and gas reserves. There are no new nuclear plants under construction in Canada or the United States. Demand for oil has been steadily rising, and our major future supply—the Alberta oil sands—is unbelievably costly to mine, consuming billions of dollars, billions of litres of fresh water, and leaving thousands of acres of devastation in its wake, along with toxic lakes that will certainly never clear in our lifetimes. In addition, Canada's oil sands are the greatest source of this nation's greenhouse gas emissions, which are the direct cause of the climate change which threatens our economy and our very way of life, as well as the homes and livelihood of hundreds of millions of people in other lands.

Consider these few words of description on the oil sands development, from an article in the *New York Times*:

> Deep craters wider than football fields are being dug out of the pine and spruce forests and muskeg swamps by many of the largest multinational oil companies. Huge refineries that burn natural gas to refine the excavated gooey sands into synthetic oil are spreading where wolves and coyotes once roamed.

Beside the mining pits, propane cannons and scarecrows installed by the companies shoo away migrating birds from giant toxic lakes filled with water that was used in the process that separates oil sands from clay and dirt.

About 82,000 acres of forest and wetlands have been cleared or otherwise disturbed since development of oil sands began in earnest here in the late 1960s, and that is just the start. It is estimated that the current daily production of just over one million barrels of oil—the equivalent of Texas' daily production, and 5 percent of the United States' daily consumption—will triple by 2015 and sextuple by 2030. The pockets of oil sands in northern Alberta—which all together equal the size of Florida—are only beginning to be developed.

"There are no moose, no rabbits, no squirrels anymore," complained Howard Lacorde, 59, a Cree trapper whose trapline has been interrupted by a new oil sands project developed by Canadian Natural Resources. "The land is dead," he added, shaking in anger, as he walked through a construction site that was once his trapline.

A barrel of oil sucked out of northern Alberta's sands causes three times more GHG to be emitted than the production of conventional crude, and consumes three to five barrels of water from the Athabaska River, as opposed to no water conventionally. Obviously, living off fossil fuels extracted at enormous cost to the environment itself is hardly a viable and sustainable, or politically acceptable, long-term solution. Get set for dramatic changes. Get real estate which can cope.

Home-building technologies now exist to produce houses that take 40 per cent less water and 30 per cent less energy. When put together in factories, such as the one operated outside Toronto by Mattamy Homes, the onsite waste generated in the construction process can be more than halved.

Progressive builders across Canada and the U.S. have been taking part of programs with names like LEED (Leadership in

Energy and Environmental Design) and Built Green, which are going far beyond switching light bulbs, low-flow washers and taps and programmable thermostats. At the same time, Canada Mortgage and Housing Corp. is offering a break on mortgage insurance to buyers of green homes, dropping the cost of premiums by 10 per cent and extending amortization coverage up to forty years. Last year more than 400 American builders turned their backs on conventional homes and joined a pilot project to create structures which slash energy needs, and that has now been followed by a handful of Canadian companies. This is an unstoppable trend, and wise buyers will demand a host of features, including:

- High-efficiency windows, doors and furnaces
- Hot water thermal panels
- Geothermal heating units
- Insulated-concrete foundations
- Rainwater collection, for lawn watering and other uses
- Native plants for landscaping
- Greywater (showers, dishwashers and laundry) re-use systems
- Solar heating
- Permeable surface driveways
- Window and door placement to maximize heat, cut hydro use
- Recycled "stone" counters and eco-friendly bamboo flooring
- Paints and adhesives low in volatile organic compounds

Also value self-sufficiency. The odds mount that governments may not be able to manage the challenges of climate change, or be too slow and unresponsive to mitigate their effects. As discussed in Chapter Four, the possibility of managed collapse exists within a few years. Evidence is clear the world cannot sustain endless growth; that overly-complex societies inevitably break down; and that environmental conditions will create challenges we are wholly unprepared for.

If another blackout, similar to that which paralyzed eastern North America in the summer of 2003, were to occur—this one lasting for weeks, or months, not hours—would you be able to function? What would you do for water, heat and electricity? Food, cash, gasoline?

None of us wish to contemplate such an event, but why not seek some insurance against it happening? Your real estate's an obvious place to start.

Geothermal heating, a woodstove or gas fireplace can provide heat. Passive heating through window placement and thermal walls can help. Solar panels or coils can keep the water in your heater tank warm. A gasoline, natural gas or propane-fired generator can replace grid-provided power. A garden makes complete sense to provide fresh greens, vegetables and crops that can be pickled or dried. Fruit trees give the same shade as maples or birch, and yet can help feed your family.

In the summer of 2007 I installed a gasoline-powered generator at a property I'd recently bought, and learned two things: The price of these units has plunged, and I was able to secure a unit that has a heated battery, electric start, giving ten hours of power on a small amount of fuel and replacing the entire load for a 1,000-square-foot residence, for less than $3,000—including installation, new panel box and breakers, buried cabling and a separate, high-security building to house it in. I also learned that, very quietly and out of the eye of the mainstream media, demand for this equipment has been surging.

I'd say this is just the tip.

KEEP REAL ESTATE IN PERSPECTIVE

If there's a giant lesson to learn from those poor souls in the United States, sitting on houses worth $300,000, or $1.3 million, and unable to get rid of them, this is it: Diversity. Far too many people who became caught up in the housing bubble in the U.S. and the real estate froth in this country put an alarming amount of their net worth into a single asset. Current conditions should tell you exactly why this is a very dangerous path to be on.

In retirement, don't have more than a third of your net worth in real estate. If you exceed that, then bail out, downsize and invest in other assets. Understand that the older you get, the more problematic real estate becomes, since it's illiquid—expensive to buy and often agony to unload. Sometimes it takes a long and expensive time until that greater fool comes along.

Also realize that rapidly rising home prices are the exception, not the norm. I've explained why this particular bubble market took place and, equally, why it cannot last. That illustrates that real estate is not the most stable place to dump your money. In fact, the stock market—viewed by most Canadians as the epitome of volatility and risk—has a much more predictable long-term track record that, say, houses in the Shaughnessy neighbourhood of Vancouver.

Thinking of buying a second home? Don't.

Cottages by the sea, cabins by the lake and farms with a pond may tug at your soul, but your soul can rent instead of tying up precious capital in some of the most changeable real estate. In declining markets, which we are entering and will be in for some time, secondary real estate such as recreational properties usually takes an early hit and sinks in value. The reason: overextended investors have a habit of dumping the place in the country first, rather than their urban home. At the same time, the number of potential buyers shrinks, and banks are less inclined to lend money for seasonal residences. Right now, just a bad idea.

Property in the US? Are you kidding?

There's a reason realtors in Florida, Arizona, Washington state and northern California have loonies in their eyes when they think of Canadians. These days American web sites, newspaper ads and direct mail are all targeting Canucks who have been juiced up by the at-par currency, and blinded by the myopic Canadian belief that our real estate market is bulletproof.

Do we think Americans are idiots? When US buyers in California, for example, are staying away from housing in droves, causing sales to drop by a fifth and prices to tumble 15 per cent—because they're convinced further declines are coming—why are we so smart to whip out the chequebook? In Florida, more than 7 per cent of all sales in 2007 were to non-residents, many of them Canadians. Property-floggers have been more than happy to fly prospective buyers down to have a look, no strings attached.

And no wonder. With Wall Street expecting a further 25 per cent plop in American housing price by the end of 2009, with that country in the grip of recession and consumers freaked out about their existing debt levels, why not target those naïve Canadians?

Remember that the sale of US real estate is subject to a with-holding tax for Canadians and that you must report rental income for an American property on both sides of the border. Mostly, though, ask yourself if you really want to be buying when all the locals are selling.

BORROW LIKE A MAN

Serious mistakes are made when people take loans to buy real estate (and most of us have no choice). Whole books have been written on mortgages, but there are just a few things to remember.

First, get a variable rate mortgage. This kind of loan has a rate which floats with the prime, while your payments are fixed for a set period of time. That means when rates change, a varying amount of you payment goes for interest or principal repayment—higher rates mean more interest and lower ones mean more principal.

Most first-time buyers and a preponderance of women borrowers opt for fixed-rate mortgages (not variable), which are most costly but offer certainty. Don't fall for it. Given economic turmoil, US recession, the real estate decline and general global growth weakness, rates are coming down. Go variable. You will save big.

Second, do not take a forty-year amortization. If you need to sink to this level, then you are buying too much real estate at too great a cost. By extending the repayment period from the normal twenty-five to forty years you are—as I have already shown—grossly increasing your overall debt and slowing your equity build-up to an absolute embarrassing trickle.

Instead, you should be shorting the am as much as possible. Granted, your monthly payments will be higher, but the loan will be repaid in a fraction of the time, and the amount of your overall debt hacked in size. By the way, amortization is French for "killed off." The best mortgage is, indeed, mort.

Third, use every trick you can to speed the repayment process, since this saves bundles of money. One is to make pre-payments, lump sum payments, whenever your lender allows it—typically up to 10 per cent or 15 per cent of the loan once a year. Another is to increase monthly payments over the required amount, with the surplus coming right off the principal outstanding.

The best method of mortgagicide I know is to dump your monthly payments and replace them with weekly ones. By accelerating payments to this frequency, you will pay off the loan in a shockingly short period of time and save tens of thousands, maybe hundreds of thousands, in interest. Take the usual monthly payment, divide it by four, and arrange with your bank to have that taken from you account every seven days. By doing so, you'll be making the equivalent of one extra monthly payment a year, with excellent results. By quickening the reduction of the principal, you slow the accumulation of new interest and see a dramatic increase in equity. This is exactly the opposite of what happens when you take a forty-year amortization.

Finally when it comes to taking a mortgage, realize that recent changes making it easier and less financially onerous are also seducing many people into real estate they perhaps should not own, and debt they may well never escape. Despite my best efforts on the House of Commons finance committee, the federal government has allowed those forty-year loans, and dropped levels for minimum down payments. It used to take a 25 per cent deposit on a home to avoid having high-ratio mortgage insurance, but that's now been scaled back to 20 per cent. Meanwhile at least one mortgage insurer has a product allowing just a 3 per cent down payment (and 97 per cent financing), with payment spread over forty years. This is said to be aimed at Toronto buyers, where the city's own new land transfer tax is preventing many first-time buyers from meeting the former 5 per cent threshold. And CMHC has made life easier for the self-employed, by offering simplified insurance allowing them to buy homes with 5 per cent down, no proof of income, and payments over four decades.

All of this should give new proof that the cult of real estate remains at dangerous levels in Canada. While dissing credit-happy Americans on one hand, dismissing their battered housing market as being unique and contained, Canadians on the other hand are careening down the same road of painless purchases and easy mortgage money. Can the final destination be much different?

By lower down payments from 25 per cent to 20 per cent to 5 per cent, to 3 per cent and zero, while lengthening repayments from twenty-five to forty years we're lowering the bar to home ownership and masking affordability. Maybe not unwise moves at the beginning of a real estate bull market, allowing more people to enjoy the ride and build wealth—but when prices have already hit a record high and housing prices have detached from incomes, this could all end badly.

FOR EVERYONE: HOW ABOUT A REAL ESTATE REALITY CHECK?

"The whole economy has been built on real estate. When the music stops, what is left?"

— John Baen, real estate professor, University of North Texas

The U.S. Federal Reserve confirmed in early 2008 that American real estate was going through its worst period in fifty years. But local agents knew that already. In some areas of Florida and

California, two-thirds of all agents hadn't sold a single property in the past year. More than twenty thousand agents quit the business in 2007 in those two states alone. In North Texas, resales fell by 18 per cent in September of 2007, by 13 per cent the following month, another 15 per cent in November, and tanked 25 per cent in December. The nation's biggest mortgage lender, Countrywide, laid off 10,986 employees in the last six months of 2007 alone. In two days in January 2008, its publicly-traded stock lost a third of its value amid rumours the company would soon be bankrupt.

Days later the teetering enterprise was taken over in a $4 billion deal by Bank of America, which was gambling heavily the mortgage portfolio would not disintegrate further.

In Toronto, meanwhile, Royal LePage announced late-2007 housing sales, and declared it to be the best year ever. That was echoed days later by the Toronto Real Estate Board, which reported a slew of buyers had snapped up homes in the final month of the year in a bid to escape the looming new and potentially devastating local land transfer tax. In their haste, they'd driven the price of houses even higher. Yearly sales were up 12 per cent, and prices ahead 7 per cent. The average cost of a standard two-storey home in Toronto crossed the $500,000 mark for the first time, while in midtown Toronto the same home averaged $1.2 million. Household incomes were unchanged, according to Statistics Canada, at less than $65,000. The average family could only dream of affording the average home, or accept a historic level of debt to get one.

As I asked earlier, what's wrong with this picture? How do housing experts and Canadian bank economists seriously believe these experiences can stay, in the buzzword of the times, "decoupled"? For a host of reasons we've discussed, Americans allowed real estate to become the base building material of the post 9/11 economy. The resulting massive asset inflation burst with predictable consequences. Clearly the same is happening in Canada. Full compliance from our financial institutions and the same

Denying the undeniable?

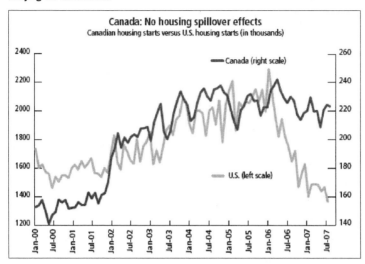

Canada: No housing spillover effects
Canadian housing starts versus U.S. housing starts (in thousands)

Many "expert" Canadian commentators have spun hard that this country, and its robust housing market, will prove to be immune to the real estate melt south of the border, as this bank-drawn chart indicates. This could be the epitome of wishful thinking.
— Datastream

benign neglect of regulators and policy-makers has pushed it along to the same bubble status. After all, when an 80-year-old brick house on a 30-foot garageless urban lot, built to subdivision standards two generations ago now changes hands for more than a million dollars, the new normal cannot last.

But while realtors gush about unseen and unparalleled heights for sales and prices, investors and consumers are told, incredibly, this is no rerun of the American experience. As clients of the private wealth management practice of one major bank were instructed, "One of the most important differences between the two countries is their housing markets. Canada has not experienced the rapid escalation in prices that the U.S. has seen over the past decade. Home prices in Canada today are in line with historical values, and housing activity has been steady."

That is hard to believe in, say, Saskatoon, where the price of the average detached bungalow increased in 2007 by 52.4 per cent, while condo values soared 49 per cent (local broker Mike

Duggleby gave this advice to the readers of the *Leader-Post* who might be thinking of buying, "Do it as soon as you can."). Or in Kelowna, where the average home price in 2007 shot ahead 19 per cent, and lakeside homes which fetched $200,000 in 2002 are now worth $1 million. Or in Vancouver, where overall prices rose 12 per cent last year, putting the average detached bungalow at $795,250, out of reach of an estimated 95 per cent of the city's inhabitants.

Are such numbers, "in line with historical values"? Let's hope not. If this isn't asset inflation, it's hard to know what is. Rather than sound concern about a real estate dependency growing as quickly in Canadian society as it did south of the border, we have a cadre of self-serving experts pushing more air into the bubble—destined only to make the inevitable more painful, more widely felt.

Given that, smart people will diversify. Quickly.

Statistics scream that this is a time to be selling real estate, not buying—unless buyers understand what they get their hands on now should be held for years, not months. The days of *Flip This House* are over and done. It's time for real estate to be viewed not just as an investment asset, but as a home, sanctuary and shelter from events to come.

As mentioned, get rid of housing with no future—McMansions, energy-burners, sprawling suburbans and anything you don't want to be lost in if the lights go out. The days for attracting a greater fool to come and pay you money for such elephants are numbered.

More importantly, do not over-invest in housing, as most of your friends, neighbours, colleagues at work and family members have. With well over four of every five dollars we have, buried in real estate, Canadians are hugely at risk of losing billions in the inevitable market correction which, I've explained, could last for years, perhaps decades. That wealth is at considerable risk, with real estate values now sitting at record levels and home ownership rates reaching the saturation point. Where do we expect the next set of fools to come from? Most affected will be those who have a small amount of equity and a whopping pile of mortgage debt, and folks who need to convert bricks-and-mortar riches into actual cash. In other words, first-time buyers lured into homes they should never have purchased, and the retiring boomers who have failed the test of diversification.

So, get out of houses with no future. List, sell, downsize, rent, wait. Vow never again to put so many of your priceless eggs in one basket. Understand that real estate's fundamentally no different that the stock market, moving quickly on emotion, rumour, headline or word-of-mouth. There is nothing innately stable, predictable or eternal about it. And those who confuse living with investing, a home with a commodity, or fail to see the obvious dangers to real property going forward, will regret their myopia.

Your real estate holdings should, on average, comprise a third of your net worth, once mortgage debt has been stripped from your personal balance sheet. If you exceed that, take action. If you do not know how to achieve the proper level of diversification, then get help. Learn what kinds of financial assets can spread your risk, give you growth and income and which, unlike real estate, are highly liquid and flexible. It doesn't take an agent, advertising, a sign at the end of your driveway and people tromping through your house for weeks, or months, to sell a stock, bond or mutual fund.

For more than a decade I have given my investible assets over to a professional money manager. In return for a relatively small annual fee, based on the size of the portfolio, my guy worries about my money every day, buying and selling and holding stocks, bonds and cash. He sends me monthly reports, tabulates annual tax liabilities and removes from me all responsibility for watching markets and picking worthy securities. The return has been consistently double the inflation rate—not as spectacular as bungalows in Saskatoon—but adequate and predictable enough. Also important, he understands my financial requirements now and into the future, based on my age and available sources of income. Rather than slapping all my money into houses or land, hoping for the best and praying I can liquidate when I need the cash, I have the instant ability to sell and take into income what I might need.

Diversification is the key to financial survival in an increasingly uncertain world. We have no concrete idea what will transpire, but the trends are obvious. People won't continue to invest in assets they cannot afford, while our complex and unequal society moves closer each day to some kind of managed collapse. It may be gentle, maybe not. In any case, you will have to live in it, and through it. Be prepared.

While a personal portfolio manager is one option—and such people are not difficult to find—investors wishing to get off the real estate juggernaut and onto firmer ground have many other choices. Independent financial advisors are available in most communities, and will typically help you with investments, insurance, debt management, estate planning and tax exposure. Accountants are handy for business owners who face complex issues of tax, succession and integration with personal assets— but are not recommended as sources of investment information.

The range of asset choices is daunting—from the easily-discounted (guaranteed investment certificates and savings bonds), to those too dangerous for most of us to touch (derivatives, currency trading) and the essential (equities, mutual funds, bonds, Treasury bills). You can be a value investor, or a growth investor or a contrarian; engage in short-selling or concentrate on buy-and-hold.

But while diversification is the holy grail, most of us do not get there on our own. Personal financial planning is not easy or quick to master, and picking appropriate investments is not less difficult that repairing your hard drive or your pancreas. This is no place for amateurs yet, sadly, legions among us trust nobody, and struggle to do it ourselves, using no-load mutual funds or online discount brokerages. Bad decision.

Surveys consistently show most Canadians fear they will lack enough money on which to retire, and they're right. With life expectancy increasing as never before, we risk running out of money far more than losing it in a bad investment. Half of us are making no RRSP contributions, in large part because we have every available dollar trapped within the walls of houses, or devoted to mortgage debt service payments. Collectively, we are so far behind in our retirement savings contributions we likely will never catch up. We have billions invested in assets, like Canada Savings Bonds, which give a negative real return, while at the same time throwing money at things which hit new lunatic highs, like gold bullion.

This is behaviour almost guaranteed to cause financial heartache. But none is worse than our misdirected and misinformed love affair with houses. We invest in real estate, almost without exception, devoid of impartial or independent advice. Instead of working with an advisor who is compensated over time by the real growth in our diversified portfolio—as a manager or advisor is—we employ an agent who's paid a one-time commission payment on the closing of a deal.

Ensure you never confuse a realtor with a financial advisor. Agents are focused on one asset only, not your entire portfolio of assets or your lifelong accumulation of wealth. And so it should be. But you need more help. Real estate assets must fit into an overall financial portfolio, and never be a substitute for those other things which can provide steady growth and liquidity.

The bottom line for millions of us with houses is stark: Will all the money there be safe, or at risk? If the market does decline, will it recover? Do I need to take action to protect myself and my family? What should I expect? Will I be able to get at my money when I need it? When time is not on my side?

Clear answers elude us. Few people in Boston, where home values doubled between 1997 and 2007, would have then expected, without warning, the worst market decline since 1958. I trust nobody in Vancouver, Kelowna, Saskatoon or Toronto expects that, either.

AFTERWORD

REAL ESTATE'S FORMED an important part of my life, and my portfolio, since I built my first home, complete, for less than I paid for my current car. If you gained the impression reading this book that housing is on my scratch list, let me correct that. I love real estate.

Most of my properties have made me money. But not all. There were recessions in the seventies and the nineties, and I was caught in both. There were booms in the eighties and in the first few years of the new Century, and I scored in those. As I write this, I have two owned homes, one urban and one lakeside, one rental home near Parliament and a commercial property outside Toronto with a binding offer on it—the last unit in a portfolio of investment real estate. Over the past three years my personal priorities have been to reduce real estate exposure, pay off debt, secure housing appropriate for the times I expect to arrive and stay diversified and flexible.

It took a concerted effort to achieve that. Selling a suburban trophy house took, as I've mentioned, a shockingly long time. Finding a home with the qualities I sought—character exterior, urban location, new infrastructure, open concept, energy-efficient, under 2,000 square feet, enough property for food options, on public transit, generator-ready, correctly priced—ended up taking a full year. I was determined to reduce my footprint and my energy consumption, while buying the kind of real estate I'm convinced has a strong future and will appreciate in value even as the general market tanks. It is what everybody will want.

This effort involved marketing a home, buying one in the midst of that process, packing and relocation, all while being busy doing other things and travelling the country. It's not easy, but real estate seldom is. That's why so many of us drag our feet, and aren't proactive, even when we know it's the right thing to do.

As for this book, without a doubt it will be attacked and panned by many who disagree with the message. The criticism I can handle (politician, remember?), but my hope is that a few key thoughts get through to Canadians who need to hear them.

I spent some time researching the real estate disaster unfolding to the south of us, determining the causes and ascertaining if they ultimately applied to us. They do. The first American national housing collapse since the Great Depression was not caused by giving dodgy mortgages to unworthy people. That may have been a factor, but it was certainly not the catalyst. If there's any one villain, it's more likely to be legendary central banker Alan Greenspan, who unleashed an orgy of debt with rock-bottom interest rates, than the guy who moved from trailer park to McMansion.

The real damage from subprime mortgages was in the financial sector, where it has yet to work through fully. The crash in real estate was, in contrast, the work of desperate buyers and greedy sellers. They caused an asset inflation fuelled by a wave of cheap money, but really created by mania. The boom became a bubble and, like all the others man has known, it burst. It may have been foolish to get caught up, but millions did.

Canadians are not paying attention if they believe we have become "decoupled" from this. Prices here, too, have escalated wildly. Here, too, the average family can no longer afford the average home. Here, too, innovation and creative mortgage products have lowered the bar to ownership and masked rising prices. Here, too, we have industry experts giving a distorted view of the market.

Meanwhile, both countries face an inevitable downturn in the economic cycle after a decade and a half of advance. We both have aging populations and a giant wave of new retirees who are house-rich (or were) and cash-poor. We all face the unknown and troubling consequences of abusing our planet for longer than it could take it. And we both live in more complex societies than have ever existed before, where self-reliance and rugged individualism have been unwisely ditched.

My views may be prescient or be proven wrong. Regardless, there will be a greater fool.

How to contact the Author

- **To discuss the ideas and statements in this book, for a daily update and open-comment blog, forum and breaking news**
Garth Turner's blog on real estate trends, developments, opportunities and dangers is written directly by the author, with daily entries and an opportunity for all visitors to post comments. The site also contains more information on the author; reviews and comments on this book; and the latest breaking news on homes and housing.

www.GreaterFool.ca

- **To send a comment directly to Garth Turner**
This personal email address will put you in touch immediately.

garth@garth.ca

- **To arrange a live appearance, presentation or seminar to your group.**
Garth Turner is one of the country's most experienced, exciting and knowledgeable public speakers. He has entertained and motivated audiences across North America, and is pleased to consider a live appearance for keynote addresses, public or private seminars, client workshops, industry or consumer shows, conventions and community groups. You may reach him by phone or email:

(416) 346-0086

garth@garth.ca